e´xcellence *n.* surpassing merit; thing in which person etc. excels. [ME f. OF, or f. L *excellentia* (as prec.; see -ENCE)]

clŭb[1] *n.* **1.** stick with one thick (INDIAN *clubs*); stick used in gam etc.) structure or organ with kn congenitally distorted foot; ~-r with upright spikes of spore-cases cabbages etc. with swelling a playing-card of suit (~s) denote association of persons united interest, usu. meeting periodicall (*Alpine*, *golf*, *yacht*, *club*) or socia pregnant; **on the ~**, (colloq.) ir below); body of persons combine and having premises for resort residence, etc., (||~**'land**, St. Ja similar area, where many clubs ber of one or more clubs; *~ sa with two layers of filling betweer or bread); ~(**'house**), premises of persons, nations, etc., hav

The Annual of the
Type Directors Club
45th Exhibition
Watson-Guptill Publications/New York

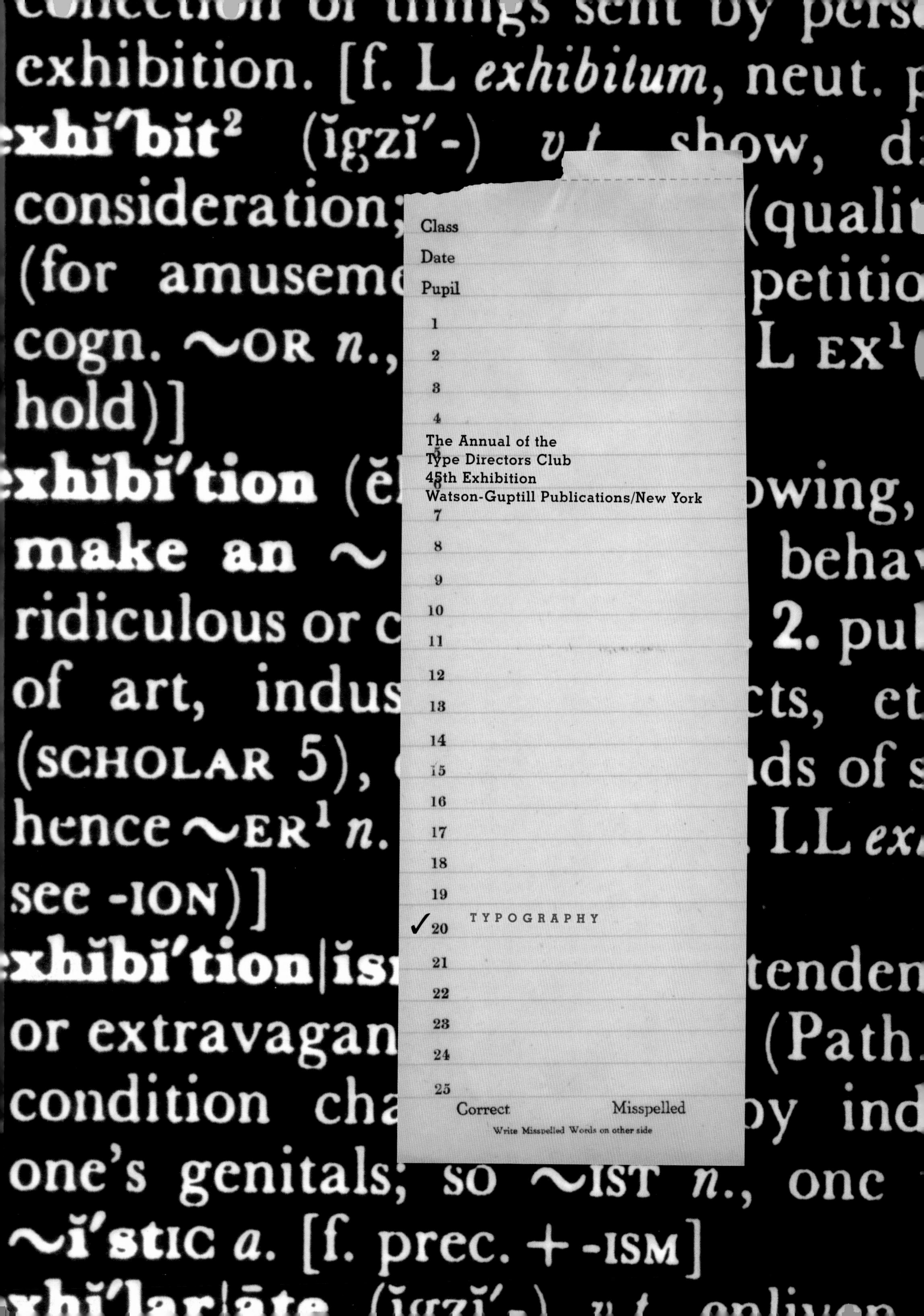

Class

Date

Pupil

1

2

3

4

5

6

7

8

9

10

11

12

13

14

15

16

17

18

19

✓ 20   TYPOGRAPHY

21

22

23

24

25

Correct   Misspelled

Write Misspelled Words on other side

First published in 1999
in the United States by
Watson-Guptill Publications,
a division of BPI
Communications, Inc.,
1515 Broadway,
New York, NY 10036

The Library of Congress
has cataloged this serial
title as follows:
Typography (Type Directors
Club [U.S.]) Typography:
the annual of the Type
Directors Club.—/—
New York: Watson-Guptill
Publications, 1980–
v.ill; 29 cm

Annual.
ISSN 0275-6870 =
Typography (New York, NY)
1. Printing, Practical—
Periodicals.
2. Graphic arts—periodicals.
1. Type Directors Club (U.S.)
z243.A2T9a 686.2'24 81-640363
AACR 2 MARC-S
Library of Congress [8605]

Manufactured in Hong Kong

ISBN 0-8230-5555-8

1 2 3 4 5 / 03 02 01 00 99

ACKNOWLEDGMENTS

The Type Directors Club gratefully
acknowledges the following for
their support and contributions to
the success of TDC45 and TDC²:

Design: Carin Goldberg and
Mary Belibasakis,
Carin Goldberg Design

Exhibition Facilities: The Aronson
Galleries, Parsons School of Design
Judging Facilities: School of Visual Arts
Chairmen's and Judges' Photos: Keith
Trumbo

TDC45 Competition (call for entries):
Design: Carin Goldberg
Printer: The Hennegan Press
Prepress: Neenah Paper
Separations: A to A Graphic
Services, Inc.

TDC² Competition (call for entries):
Design: Paul Shaw
Printer: Print International
Prepress: A to A Graphic
Services, Inc.
Paper: The Ace Group
and Lindemeyr Munroe

For Watson-Guptill Publications:
Senior Editor: Marian Appellof
Associate Editor: Alison Hagge
Design Coordinator: Jay Anning
Production Manager: Ellen Greene

Carin Goldberg would like to
thank the Type Directors Club and
Watson-Guptill Publications for the
opportunity to design this book with
complete trust and creative freedom.

The principal typeface used
in the composition of
TYPOGRAPHY 20 is Stymie.

Contents

WORDS OF WISDOM.

So where would we be without typography? To use the cooking analogy, the designer's choice of a specific typeface for a specific piece is very similar to a chef's selection of just the right seasoning for his or her culinary creation. Yes, there are many ways to prepare the same dish, but that special spice—that special flavor—is what differentiates the gourmet from the average. The same goes for type. While there are many typefaces to choose from (Oh my God, there are so many!), what makes one typeface more appropriate than another for a certain project? What makes the excellent work stand out above the rest?

For the past forty-five years, the Type Directors Club has been presenting the year's best of the best. Each annual, each show, has become a record—a capsule of the best work the design and advertising communities have offered that year. With this high criterion in mind, I set out to find seven judges who I felt would best select work that would illustrate the diversity in design that exists today. I wanted seven people with different backgrounds—each coming to the table with a slightly different perspective on type and design.

It was a pleasure to work with such an elite jury. Drew Hodges, John Korpics, Bill Oberlander, John Parham, Stefan Sagmeister, Jennifer Sterling, and Niklaus Troxler all did a fantastic job judging this show. I am proud to say that this jury, along with Carin Goldberg (the esteemed book jacket designer whom I selected to design the call and this annual), drew the largest number of entries in the history of the Type Directors Club. TDC45 presents 261 pieces selected by this jury that we all feel illustrate the high standard of graphic design and typography existing today.

ADAM GREISS is a design consultant based in New York City. He received his BFA from the School of Visual Arts, with a major in Graphic Design/Media Communications. For the past two years Mr. Greiss has been an instructor of typography and graphic design at the School of Visual Arts, and he previously taught for five years at Parsons School of Design.

Over the past thirteen years Mr. Greiss has been responsible for creating award-winning corporate identities, corporate capabilities brochures, annual reports, advertising, packaging, publications, and Web sites for some of the leaders in American industry.

In 1988 Mr. Greiss joined Michael Aron and Company as a graphic designer. He completed his role with the company after four years as Senior Designer. In 1992 Mr. Greiss opened his own firm, Adam Greiss Design, Inc., where he served as President. In 1997, after five years of running his own business, he became tired of being primarily a businessman and longed for being creative once again. At this time he joined The O Group, Inc. as Creative Director and has since moved on to consulting.

Mr. Greiss's work has received more than forty-five national and international awards, including AIGA, Type Directors Club, Graphis, Print Regional, Print's Best Logos and Symbols, Society of Publication Designers, American Corporate Identity, Creativity, and the American Design awards.

Mr. Greiss's work is in the permanent collection of the Library of Congress. His published works have appeared in numerous graphic design books as well as THE GRAPHIC DESIGN PORTFOLIO by Paula Scher and YOU THINK YOU'VE GOT IT BAD?, which he co-authored (as illustrator) with William J. Ciesla, Jr. He has also been written up in the following publications: GRAPHIS, GRAPHIC DESIGN: USA, ADWEEK, REAL ESTATE WEEKLY, and REAL ESTATE NEW YORK.

Mr. Greiss has guest lectured about graphic design at leading universities as well as in the New York public school system.

Mr. Greiss's membership affiliations include the Type Directors Club (of which he has also served on the Board of Directors for four years), American Institute of Graphic Arts (AIGA), and National Academy of Recording Arts and Sciences (NARAS), the presenters of the Grammy Awards.

DREW HODGES

Drew Hodges is Creative Director of Spot Design and SpotCo. Spot Design, established in 1987, is a design studio that specializes in work for the entertainment industry.

Spot Design's client list includes DreamWorks, ABC Television, Nickelodeon, MTV Networks, Calvin Klein, Comedy Central, Geffen Records, Sony Music, BMG Records, Swatch Watch, TV Land, and Paramount Pictures.

SpotCo., established in 1997, is a full-service advertising agency that specializes in the theater industry. Clients include the Broadway and international productions of RENT, THE DIARY OF ANNE FRANK, ANNIE GET YOUR GUN, CHICAGO, Sandra Bernhard's I'M STILL HERE, DAMN IT!, John Leguizamo's FREAK, THE BLUE ROOM with Nicole Kidman, DE LA GUARDA, the 1997 and 1998 Tony Awards, and AMY'S VIEW with Dame Judi Dench.

BILL OBERLANDER

Bill Oberlander is Managing Partner/Executive Creative Director of Kirsenbau Bond & Partners. Bill is responsible for every communication piece that leaves t agency. He oversees the entire creative staff, as well as the design, Internet, ar direct-response departments. A devout art director, Bill believes that an art directo job is only half done when he/she comes up with a great campaign idea—for a gre art director knows that the graphic "look" of the ad can say as much as the wor themselves. Bill is also President of the Art Directors Club, where he recently gave t speech "Make the Logo Bigger."

In his abundant spare time, Bill adores his wife, Dale, two boys, William and Bertra and dog, Louise, at their home in New York City.

JOHN KORPICS

John Korpics has been Design Director of ENTERTAINMENT WEEKLY for the past three years, which translates roughly to 156 issues (he has fond memories of working at a monthly magazine).

He studied design at Carnegie Mellon University and has worked for a variety of award-winning publications, including GQ, PREMIERE, MUSICIAN, and REGARDIE'S.

John has recently received the National Magazine Award for design. Turn-ons include an organized garage, Ping-Pong, and bad gas mileage. Turn-offs include faulty septic systems, WHEEL OF FORTUNE, and Corvinus Skyline.

John lives in Westchester County, New York, with his wife, Cathleen, their two daughters, Daisy and Ruby, and their dog, Sam.

JOHN PARHAM

As President of Parham Santana, John Parham helms a staff of twenty and supervises all new business, sales, and marketing efforts. Also, he is one of the company's four creative directors and an active consultant to clients. A native of Kentucky, John earned his BA from the University of Louisville. In 1980, John traveled to Brooklyn, where he entered the graduate program in Communication Arts at Pratt Institute. In 1985 he and his wife, Maruchi Santana, founded Parham Santana, a marketing and creative firm. The company has an international client list based in the licensing, entertainment, electronic, consumer product, and retail industries. John is passionate about his company, his family, New York City, and the Brooklyn brownstone where he lives with Maruchi and their three bilingual children.

STEFAN SAGMEISTER

Stefan Sagmeister, a native of Austria, received h MFA in graphic design from the University of Applie Arts in Vienna and, as a Fulbright scholar, a master degree from Pratt Institute in New York.

Following stints at M&Co in New York and as Creati Director at the Hong Kong branch of the advertisin agency Leo Burnett, Sagmeister formed the New Yor based Sagmeister, Inc., in 1993.

He has designed graphics and packaging for th Rolling Stones, David Byrne, Lou Reed, Aerosmith, ar Pat Metheny.

His work has been nominated four times for th Grammy Awards and has won most internation design awards.

He lives in New York and loves Anni.

Judges

JENNIFER STERLING

Jennifer Sterling is principal of Sterling Design, which is based in San Francisco. The firm specializes in the design of packaging, books, collateral communications, products, branding, and multimedia.

Her work has been published in GRAPHIS, COMMUNICATION ARTS, CRITIQUE, PRINT, HOW, and I.D.'S DESIGN REVIEW; the annuals of the American Center for Design, Type Directors Club, and American Institute of Graphic Arts; and the publications of AR 100, Mead Annual Report Show, and the Society of Illustrators. The work of Sterling Design is also included in the permanent collection of the Library of Congress and in the San Francisco Museum of Modern Art.

Jennifer is a member of the TDC, American Center for Design, PCBA, and AIGA. She has lectured and juried for these and other organizations across the country. She is on the design faculty of California College of Arts and Crafts, where she teaches advanced typography in graphic design. Sterling Design was recognized by Graphis as one of twelve top design firms, and Jennifer was recently recognized as one of twelve designers to change design into the millennium.

NIKLAUS TROXLER

To view a Niklaus Troxler poster for a jazz concert is to physically absorb the rhythm and power of the music itself. A Troxler poster transmits its sense of the music through the eyes rather than the ears. In this computer-based age, Troxler's chosen means of expression could be seen as moving against the mainstream of current design. Ironically, though, this counterflow is giving new prominence to his work.

Troxler was born and still resides in Willisau, Switzerland. He studied graphic design and typography at the Art School of Lucerne in the mid-1960s. Since 1973 he has worked in his own graphic design studio. This year he has become a professor at the Art Academy in Stuttgart, Germany.

Niklaus has received first prizes at the Essen Poster Triennial (1987 and 1993), the Chaumont Poster Competition (1992), the Lahti Poster Biennial (1993), the first Helsinki Poster Biennial (1997), the Rzeszow Theater Poster Biennial (1997), and the Trnava Poster Triennial (1997).

He has had his work exhibited in Paris, Berlin, Frankfurt, New York, Mexico City, Venezuela, and China.

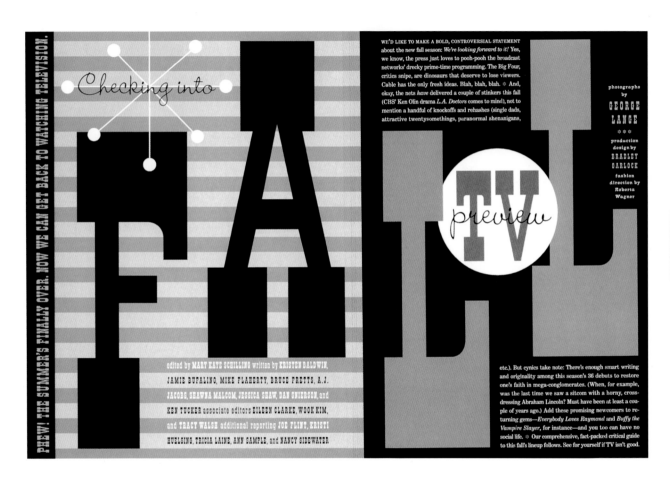

PHEW! THE SUMMER'S FINALLY OVER. NOW WE CAN GET BACK TO WATCHING TELEVISION.

Checking into

FALL

TV preview

WE'D LIKE TO MAKE A BOLD, CONTROVERSIAL STATEMENT about the new fall season: *We're looking forward to it!* Yes, we know, the press just loves to pooh-pooh the broadcast networks' drecky prime-time programming. The Big Four, critics snipe, are dinosaurs that deserve to lose viewers. Cable has the only fresh ideas. Blah, blah, blah. ❋ And, okay, the nets *have* delivered a couple of stinkers this fall (CBS' Ken Olin drama *L.A. Doctors* comes to mind), not to mention a handful of knockoffs and rehashes (single dads, attractive twentysomethings, paranormal shenanigans,

photographs by
GEORGE LANGE
❋ ❋ ❋
production design by
BRADLEY CARLOCK
fashion direction by
Roberta Wagner

etc.). But cynics take note: There's enough smart writing and originality among this season's 36 debuts to restore one's faith in mega-conglomerates. (When, for example, was the last time we saw a sitcom with a horny, cross-dressing Abraham Lincoln? Must have been at least a couple of years ago.) Add these promising newcomers to returning gems—*Everybody Loves Raymond* and *Buffy the Vampire Slayer,* for instance—and you too can have no social life. ❋ Our comprehensive, fact-packed critical guide to this fall's lineup follows. See for yourself if TV isn't good.

edited by MARY KAYE SCHILLING written by KRISTEN BALDWIN, JAMIE BUFALINO, MIKE FLAHERTY, BRUCE FRETTS, A.J. JACOBS, SHAWNA MALCOM, JESSICA SHAW, DAN SNIERSON, and KEN TUCKER associate editors EILEEN CLARKE, WOOK KIM, and TRACY WALSH additional reporting JOE FLINT, KRISTI HUELSING, TRICIA LAINE, ANN SAMPLE, and NANCY SIDEWATER

JOHN KORPICS JUDGE'S WORK

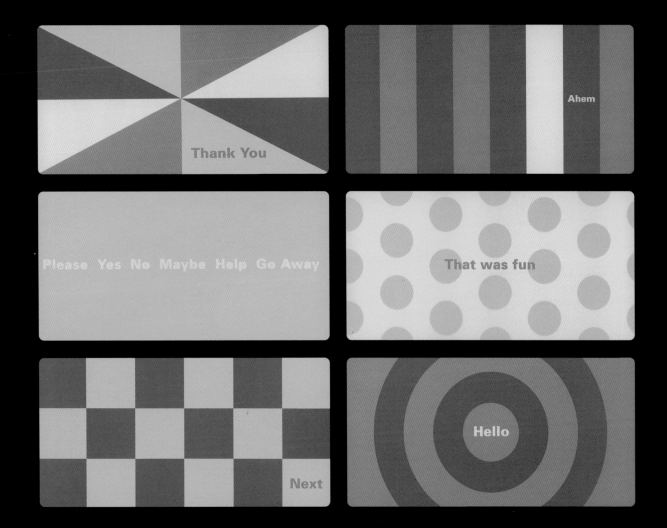

STEFAN SAGMEISTER JUDGE'S WORK

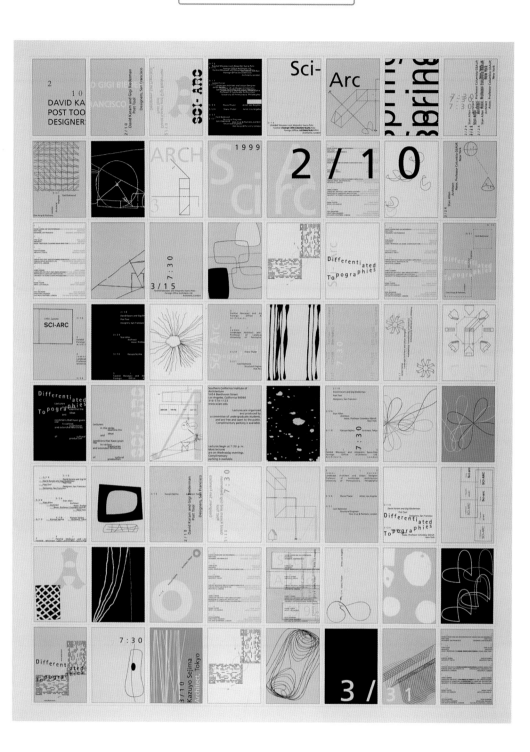

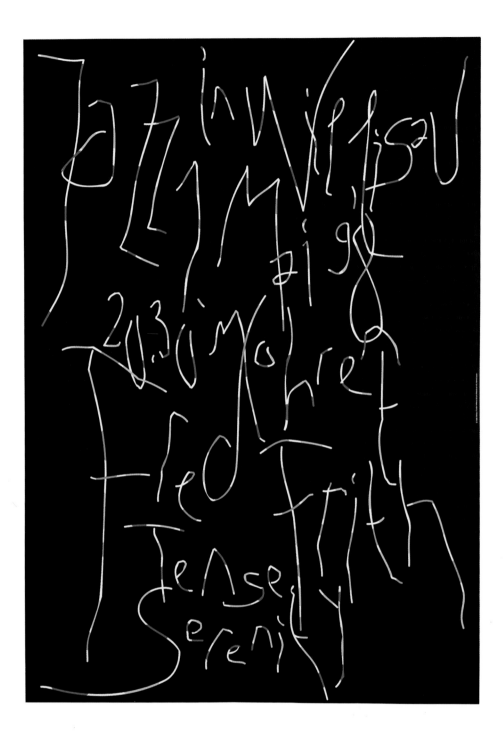

Judges' *Choices*

DREW HODGES

I chose Johnson & Wolverton's Miller Genuine Draft campaign for a wide variety of reasons. One, it seems to be more about Miller beer than about Johnson & Wolverton. I like that. Two, it actually seems to be about people's real life, only a bit heightened. I have to admit that most beer campaigns don't really fit any experience I've ever had with beer, whether it's bouncing coeds on touch football fields, or towering mountains crusting over with cool blue ice. The candor that the vernacular style seems to project makes a huge difference to me as an audience. It seems to say: "We know you. We're celebrating you, not some other guy."

The design style of so-called lifestyle products also serves as an invitation, like a party you either do or do not want to attend. People pick up the style signals you are sending them and immediately interpret whether your message is one intended for them, or whether you are actually saying: "You don't relate to this? You weren't meant to." Design is always giving a dual message: the specifics we need to say—like price, date, how it works, what it does for you, etc.—as well as a message that is more emotional. Like the feeling you get from the ad? Well then, you'll like the similar feeling you get from using the actual product, service, etc. These ads seem to be saying that drinking MGD is like having a party in a dark poolroom with the incredibly cool friends you already possess in your already incredibly cool life. I can get into that. I just wish I knew how to play pool.

Johnson & Wolverton worked with ad agency Wieden & Kennedy to produce the print component of the Miller Genuine Draft advertising campaign. The design sought to document and observe contemporary American archetypes, as well as celebrate them. Industrial mishaps and happenstance add up to a visual nonchalance, an ironic self-awareness on the brand's part. It invites the customer to drink this beer as part of a cultural ritual that belongs to a world under attack by refinements of the contemporary world. The visual language of this campaign then quotes the look of the Rust Belt as a kind of indigenous folk art. This design approach gives consumers a cultural lens for viewing the brand.

IT'S MILLER TIME

POINT OF PURCHASE

Design
Hal Wolverton and Heath
Lowe
Portland, Oregon

Lettering
Hal Wolverton, Heath Lowe,
Joe Peila, Sarah Starr, Alan
Foster, Neil Gust, Mary
Kysar, and Topher Sinkinson

Art Direction
Alicia Johnson and Hal
Wolverton

Creative Direction
Hal Wolverton and Alicia
Johnson

Photography
Terry Richardson

Agency
Wieden & Kennedy

Studio
Johnson & Wolverton

Client
Miller Brewing Co.

Principal Type
Interstate (modified)

Dimensions
18 x 24 in. (45.7 x 61 cm)

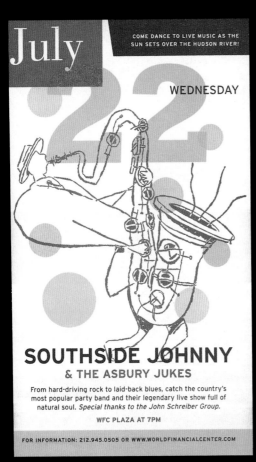

July

COME DANCE TO LIVE MUSIC AS THE
SUN SETS OVER THE HUDSON RIVER!

WEDNESDAY

22

SOUTHSIDE JOHNNY
& THE ASBURY JUKES

From hard-driving rock to laid-back blues, catch the country's
most popular party band and their legendary live show full of
natural soul. *Special thanks to the John Schreiber Group.*

WFC PLAZA AT 7PM

FOR INFORMATION: 212.945.0505 OR WWW.WORLDFINANCIALCENTER.COM

HUDSON RIVER

Festival

Arts &
Events

SUMMER 1998

July

WHOA! SWIMMING IN THE RIVER!

THURSDAY

23

Swim Across America's
HUDSON RIVER SWIM

The 26-mile relay swim from Tarrytown to the WFC's North
Cove Yacht Harbor benefits Memorial Sloan-Kettering Cancer
Center. Information: (888) SWIM-USA. Fundraising Finish Line
Party at Moran's at the World Financial Center.

FINISH LINE PARTY AT EDWARD MORAN'S BAR & GRILL AT 6PM

FOR INFORMATION: 212.945.0505 OR WWW.WORLDFINANCIALCENTER.COM

CALENDAR

Design
Lisa Yee
New York, New York

Creative Direction
Stephen Doyle

Illustration
Ward Schumaker

Production
Red Ink Productions

Studio
Doyle Partners

Client
World Financial Center Arts
and Events Program

Principal Type
Interstate, Bodoni, and
Rockwell

Dimensions
4 x 6¾ in. (10.2 x 17.1 cm)

JOHN KORPICS

If I hadn't stopped to clean my glasses, I might never have seen it. Somewhere between the zillion-colored, embossed, foil-stamped paper company entries that were reflecting light at twice the intensity of the sun, and the ten-foot-high typography lecture series posters that consisted of a single nine-foot-high Helvetica Italic character, was the Hudson River Festival calendar.

I immediately liked it because it had a function (it was a calendar), but as I looked closer, I started to see what a smart design this was. It was five inches high and about three inches wide—not necessarily the best size for getting noticed on a table next to 10,000 other entries, but the perfect size to stick in your pocket and carry around the city. Functionality to go. I liked that.

It was printed on paper that was a little thinner than the film on top of your mushroom soup. This was probably a financial decision, but I liked that also. It wasn't too precious—a mutt among the purebreds.

Doyle Partners (who designed this item) had made some smart choices. First, they utilized six alternating spot colors as the fourth color on a web press, which was a budget-savvy way to provide a variety of color treatments throughout. They also used desktop scans as final art, which made sense, since most of the pictures they had were bad anyway. But these things didn't make it special, they just made it smart.

The design was a joyous jumble of fonts, shapes, colors, rules, bursts, and big dates. When they combined all that with the rough halftones and the gracefully loose drawings of Ward Schumaker, it made each page feel like it was dancing. Rockwell, Bodoni, Interstate. They were all there. Sometimes leading, sometimes following, but always working. Nothing lined up, nothing trapped, everything surprinted everything else, and no page looked exactly alike, but at the same time it was easy to read, concise, informative, and—most importantly—FUN.

And I guess that's why I liked it. It was good to see that somebody could still have fun (and design well) on a budget. In New York, that's an achievement.

We decided to tackle the Hudson River Festival like many other challenges—one day at a time! The World Financial Center Arts and Events Program and Battery Park City Authority teamed up as a client, offering the biggest free entertainment program New York has ever seen.

This gummed calendar pad displayed the sheer volume of events (it was thick) and delivered a surprise every day with an event, interesting tidbit, or new place in the historic area to visit. High-volume illustrations by Ward Schumaker brought energy and unity to this fun, disposable ephemera. Some printing savvy was utilized to keep production costs low: we used low-resolution, in-house, and CD scans as final artwork and printed with a four-color web press (employing six alternating spot colors) onto grubby newsprint.

BILL OBERLANDER

It is difficult to separate the Balthazar typography from the many eating experiences I have had there. The first time I had dinner there, we were seated near the likes of Sandra Bernhard, Bianca Jagger, and, yes, Mr. Jerry Seinfeld. It was such a scene. But it was a great scene because if you closed your eyes and squinted your brain, you could have very easily imagined yourself not in New York, but in Paris—say, at Café Deux Magots or Brasserie La Coupole.

The place feels like the real thing—from the bakery, to the three-tiered shellfish platters, to the weathered wall mirrors, to the waiters' aprons. The typography is equally genuine—the restaurant menus, the place mats, the bar napkins, the match-boxes, the take-out menus, the wine list, the baguette bags. Everything looks utterly nineteenth-century France. It is totally convincing. I would go so far as to say that the typography is so good that it actually makes the food taste better.

Over a year ago, as I sipped a glass of wine, selected from the handsome wine list, half of my brain was asking: "Who designed all these materials—they are so well done." I was excited to see it all together in the show and delighted that it is a winner. I hope you all agree.

P.S. Did I mention that my favorite city in the world is Paris?

It began as a simple plan for a modest brasserie—a few menus and a logotype. But compulsive natures captured the effort, resulting in a New York icon.

Maniacal attention to detail governed each move and made the creation of a signature graphic statement essential.

It also made for great fun, allowing me to dive into myriad typefaces from another time and place and tap into the power of collective memory to recreate a feeling and infuse each piece with atmosphere.

The effect of the typography was further extended through the seamless integration of two-dimensional type into the three-dimensional space of architecture and food. It appears on the windows and floats on the awnings. It is pressed into the small butter cups that are brought to each table and baked into the brown crusts of fresh loaves of bread.

At Balthazar, type plays a significant role in transforming simple dining into an immersing and memorable event.

CAMPAIGN

Design
Matteo Federico Bologna
New York, New York

Art Direction
Matteo Federico Bologna

Creative Direction
Matteo Federico Bologna

Studio
Matteo Bologna Design/NY

Client
Balthazar

Principal Type
Bitstream Americana, FF
Bodoni Classics, Adobe
Akzidenz Grotesk, Font
Bureau Grotesque, and
Monotype Engravers

Dimensions
Various

POSTER

Design
Ralph Schraivogel
Zurich, Switzerland

Printer
Serigraphie Uldry
Hinterkappelen, Switzerland

Studio
Schraivogel Design

Client
Zurich Film Podium

Principal Type
Found type

Dimensions
35⅝ x 50⅜ in. (90.5 x 128 cm)

JOHN PARHAM

This poster for a Woody Allen Retrospective/Discussion is my Judge's Choice because it is so disarmingly simple. By that I mean it is immediate and direct, but as I look deeper it operates on more subtle and nuanced levels.

The success of this work begins with its economy of means. The designer reduces everything to one singular decision—the street map. And with Allen, it's got to be a New York City street map. With a map as a grid, it drives all subsequent design decisions. Where else could you put the type? Where else could you put the imagery?

But the map is not only an organizer; it's also a metaphor. It's easy to see how New York represents the body of Allen's work, and the blocks different facets of his career. And somehow the whole thing feels and looks like film—you have sequential, rectangular images with continuous borders.

As for the type, I think it's perfect and give it bonus points for not being trendy. There is no vernacular or historical reference to work through. You don't really see a typeface; you simply see information.

Yes, I'm a Woody Allen fan and was predisposed to go deep, but this piece allowed it. The work is right for a lot of reasons. It's New York, it's intellectual, it's not overproduced, it's very Woody Allen.

After I viewed, within one week, almost all of Woody Allen's films on video, I couldn't stand that face anymore. When I showed up with a purely typographical proposal for the poster, the client insisted on using a photo of Woody Allen. I knew I could not make the problem go away, so I decided to multiply it by showing his face twelve times. That the idea to use the grid of Manhattan came to me immediately made me very suspicious. However, when I finally tried it, I was surprised by the coincidence of duplicate letters in the name WOODY Allen and in the word BROADWAY. And, lazy as I am, I was very attracted to the possibility of solving all typographical problems simply and at once.

STEFAN SAGMEISTER

....

This little calendar was not only my favorite piece in the show, it's one of the best calendars I've ever seen. Designer Juli Gudehus counts down the last year in this millennium with expiration dates of food products. Simply a great idea. There's a different product going bad on every calendar sheet on every day. You recognize some of the products, shown in tight crops to make the date the hero. On January 11 the fresh butter is fresh no more, on Wednesday, September 6, the great chocolates from Demel in Vienna turn rancid. The variations of typefaces and application techniques are also incredible: there are embossed, stamped, offset-printed, letterpressed, flexi-printed, ink-jetted, and debossed expiration dates included.

Juli painstakingly collected all items, Alistair Overbruck photographed them, and the resulting round-cornered calendar, shrink-wrapped into a green Styrofoam tray, is simply breathtaking. It easily fulfills both requirements for good type: an original idea well executed.

Normally remarked with a housewife's critical fleeting glance, dates of expiration lived in the shadow—far away from any graphic design highlights and cultural affairs. Then I began to buy various odd stuff in order to get 365 expiration dates to demonstrate the countdown of the twentieth century.

Discovering expiration dates with esthetic packaging became my passion. Missing dates made me buy things nobody would ever eat. The complete collection was published as a day-by-day calendar for the last year of the millennium, packed like meat on green Styrofoam trays. It soon became a piece of desire.

This may show that one can see everyday design in a different light when it is taken out of the "normal" context. By publishing this calendar, Verlag Hermann Schmidt transformed ordinary expiration dates into pieces of typographic art.

Design
Juli Gudehus
Cologne, Germany

Art Direction
Juli Gudehus

Creative Direction
Juli Gudehus

Photography
Alistair Overbruck

Client
Verlag Hermann Schmidt
Mainz

Principal Type
Various

Dimensions
5⅛ x 3⅛ in. (13 x 8 cm)

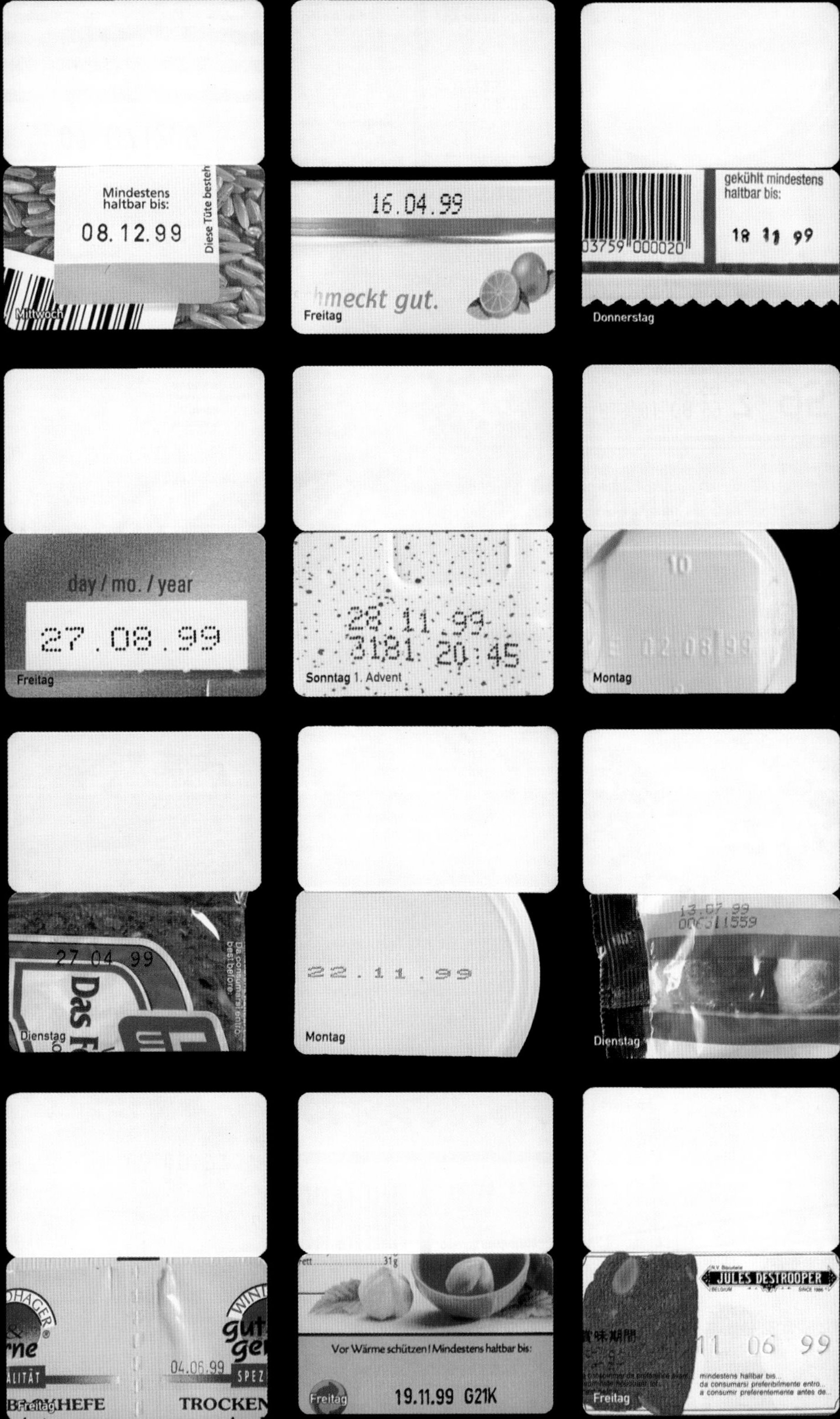

JENNIFER STERLING

It was virtually impossible to commit to the selection of one piece as my Judge's Choice. How do you choose between an elegant typographic letterpress book (that you would really like to slide off the table and into your luggage) and the work of an editorial art director that is virtually always brilliant? After I made my decision, I continued to think about it. Finally, I ran back into the room and changed my selection. I chose the typographic posters, designed and illustrated by James Victore, that denounce and "Just Say No" to Mickey. These two posters aggressively dismiss the world in which we have one clothing store, one bank, one coffee house, one design firm (Oh, now it bothers some of you), and one theme park. As James Victore states: "not everyone wants Times Square to resemble Des Moines." The posters are passionate, spontaneous, unlike anything else in the show, and made me gleeful each time I saw them. I should have snuck one off the street while they were still available.

No one travels to New York City to have the same experience (or buy the same crap) that they can have in any mall or airport. I created these posters to give a voice to the many New Yorkers who don't believe that corporations such as Disney have our best interests at heart. These two posters, as well as one created by a group of my former students, were hung around New York City and Times Square during the holiday season. We wanted to create gritty, poignant, and witty posters that would serve as a reminder that not everybody wants Times Square to resemble Des Moines.

BOOK

· · · · · · · · · · · · ·

Design
Various Student Designers
Pasadena, California

· · · · · · · · · · · · ·

Art Direction
Vance Studley

· · · · · · · · · · · · ·

Creative Direction
Vance Studley

· · · · · · · · · · · · ·

Agency
Archetype Press

· · · · · · · · · · · · ·

Studio
Art Center College of
Design

· · · · · · · · · · · · ·

Principal Type
Various foundry metal, wood,
and digital type

· · · · · · · · · · · · ·

Dimensions
8½ x 11 in. (21.6 x 27.9 cm)

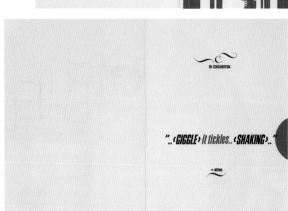

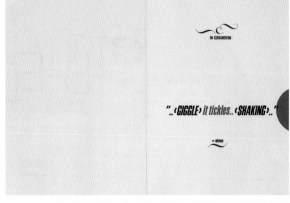

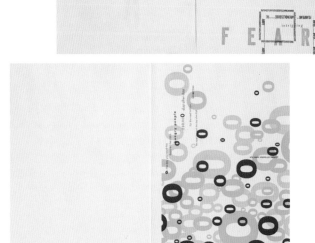

NIKLAUS TROXLER

That wonderful booklet, PRESSING ISSUES, printed upon genuine handmade paper, caught my eye as a particularly comfortable visual design within that expansive forest of jury submissions. It is a printed piece that one handles like a precious gem or an original craft object. The booklet emits warmth and embodies the identical love with which it was designed, printed, and finished. There should be more printed designs of such a lofty standard. It truly is a rose amid a flood of disposable printed material.

Nevertheless, this booklet also fascinates through its very unpretentiousness, its simplicity. Every one of those thirty-nine designers has created a page in a deeply individual graphic language, thus making an extremely personal design statement. The fact that all of the designers approached this task with great seriousness—and still made their pleasure in designing quite apparent—renders this booklet so very special.

PRESSING ISSUES is a compilation of comments, observations, and short quotes that encapsulate the social, political, and artistic dilemmas that beset us as the new millennium gradually unfolds. Purely typographic and hand-set in metal, wood, and polymer plates, each of the quotes from the designers was framed using the zone of the page as a stage for the dynamics of the letterforms and the correspondences among the words. Within Archetype Press's collection of 400 metal fonts, compositions were carefully arranged and letterpress-printed on Vandercook proof presses, combining more than sixty-five custom colors. Each book is hand-bound; the small edition consists of fifty-two copies, the work revealing type as an embodiment of our innermost thoughts.

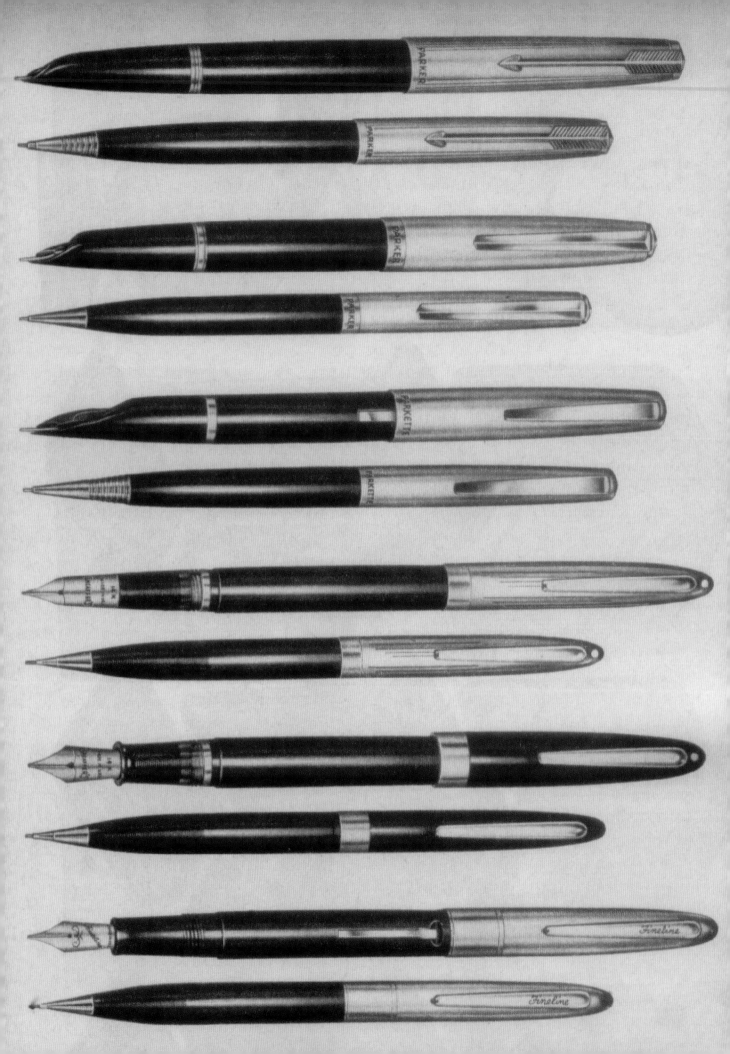

Entries

Selected

for

Typographic

Excellence

THE ART DIRECTORS CLUB OF TULSA PRESENTS
WERNER DESIGN WERKS • MINNEAPOLIS, MN
THURSDAY, MARCH 19, 1998
THE TULSA GARDEN CENTER
2435 SOUTH PEORIA AVENUE • TULSA, OK

WERNER
DESIGN
Werks | INC.

The answers lie ahead.
MOVE FORWARD.

NEW! NEW! NEW! NEW! NEW! NEW! NEW! NEW! NEW! NEW! NEW! NEW!

LOCALE
411
FIRST AVENUE NORTH

NO.
206

MPLS. MN

ZIP CODE
55401

CONVENIENTLY LOCATED NEAR
THE CORNER OF FIRST AVENUE
AND FOURTH STREET

FACSIMILE 612.338.2598

(612) 338
2550

TELEPHONE

E-MAIL WERNER@WDW.COM

OPEN

Move.

YOUR MIND

SINCE 1991

WDW

WERNER DESIGN WE
Your Design Professionals

BIG PROJECTS
SMALL PROJECT

LOGOS
STATIONERY
BOOKS
ANNUAL REPORTS
POSTERS
(THIS ONE, FOR EXAMPLE)
CATALOGS
PROMOTIONS
PACKAGING
BROCHURES

PRINTED MATERIALS
ALL SORTS

FOR EXTERNAL USE ONLY

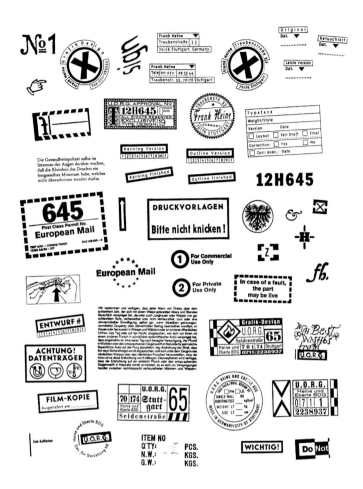

RUBBER STAMPS

Design
Frank Heine
Stuttgart, Germany

Text
Sibilla Bolay

Studio
U.O.R.G. Heine und Eberle
BDG

Principal Type
Triplex, FF Instanter, and
Erbar (modified)

Dimensions
Various

POSTER

Design
Sarah Nelson
Minneapolis, Minnesota

Art Direction
Sharon Werner

Studio
Werner Design Werks, Inc.

Client
Art Directors Club of Tulsa

Principal Type
Various

Dimensions
19 x 24 in. (48.3 x 61 cm)

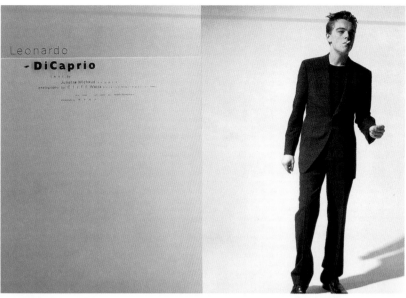

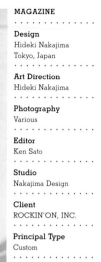

MAGAZINE

Design
Hideki Nakajima
Tokyo, Japan

Art Direction
Hideki Nakajima

Photography
Various

Editor
Ken Sato

Studio
Nakajima Design

Client
ROCKIN'ON, INC.

Principal Type
Custom

Dimensions
13 x 9⅜ in. (33 x 23.8 cm)

Though shown together here,
these six spreads were
chosen independently.

Lili Taylor | Steve Buscemi

ハーモニー・コリン

ジャン・レノ

JEAN
RÉNO

TV COMMERCIAL
. . . .

Design
Carla Bieniek
New York, New York
. . . .

Art Direction
Matthew Duntemann
. . . .

Creative Direction
Matthew Duntemann
. . . .

Animation
Carla Bieniek
. . . .

Client
TV Land
. . . .

Principal Type
Juniper, Kuenstler Script,
Neuzeit Grotesk Bold
Condensed, and Univers
Light Ultra Condensed

POSTER
. . . .

Design
Ralph Schraivogel
Zurich, Switzerland
. . . .

Printer
Serigraphie Uldry
Hinterkappelen, Switzerland
. . . .

Studio
Schraivogel Design
. . . .

Client
Zurich Film Podium
. . . .

Principal Type
3-D display letters
. . . .

Dimensions
35⅝ x 50⅜ in. (90.5 x
128 cm)

SHAKES
PEARE'S
CINEMA
APR·MAI
IM·FILM

'STUDIO 4'
NÜSCHELERSTR. II. ZÜRICH

PODIUM

LONG WHARF THEATRE
THE GIMMICK
DIRECTED BY JAYE AUSTIN-WILLIAMS
ARTISTIC DIRECTOR DOUG HUGHES
WRITTEN AND PERFORMED BY DAEL ORLANDERSMITH
CONCEIVED AND ORIGINALLY DIRECTED BY PETER ASKIN
OCT 27-DEC 6, 1998
TICKETS (203) 787-4282 OR (800) 782-8497
SNET
We go beyond the call
SPONSOR OF THE STAGE II SEASON

sucker and dry 3:09

the bit just chokes them 4:54

ZERO HOUR ZEP SI 0013 ℗© 1997 Zero Hour Records, Inc.
14 W 23rd St. NY, NY 10010 http://www.zerohour.com
Warning: All rights reserved. Unauthorized
duplication is a violation of applicable laws. 45 RPM

PACKAGING

· · · · · · · · · · · · ·

Design
Mike Joyce
New York, New York

· · · · · · · · · · · · ·

Art Direction
Mike Joyce

· · · · · · · · · · · · ·

Creative Direction
Mike Joyce

· · · · · · · · · · · · ·

Studio
Stereotype

· · · · · · · · · · · · ·

Client
Zero Hour Records and
Cursive

· · · · · · · · · · · · ·

Principal Type
Futura and Helvetica
Compressed

· · · · · · · · · · · · ·

Dimensions
7⅛ x 7⅛ in. (18.1 x 18.1 cm)

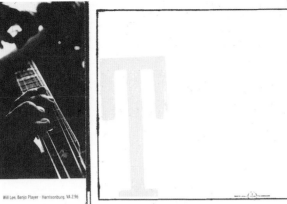

Will Lee, Banjo Player · Harrisonburg, VA 2.96

PROMOTION
. . . .

Design
Kristina DiMatteo
New York, New York
. . . .

Art Direction
Kristina DiMatteo
. . . .

Creative Direction
Carol Bobolts
. . . .

Photography
C. Taylor Crothers
. . . .

Studio
Red Herring Design
. . . .

Client
C. Taylor Crothers
. . . .

Principal Type
Interstate, Octopuss, and
various wood type
. . . .

Dimensions
9¾ x 4 in. (24.8 x 10.2 cm)

PHONE CARD
. . . .

Design
Times Pang and Lawrence
Choy
Hong Kong, China
. . . .

Art Direction
Times Pang and Lawrence
Choy
. . . .

Creative Direction
Times Pang and Lawrence
Choy
. . . .

Studio
Point-Blank Studio
. . . .

Client
New T&T Hong Kong
Limited
. . . .

Principal Type
Helvetica Neue
. . . .

Dimensions
3⅜ x 2⅛ in. (8.6 x 5.4 cm)

01 Experts in information communications: San Francisco, Berlin, London

02 London designer, principal at Research Studios, co-founder of FUSE

03 The best fonts in the world from the world's largest mail order distributor

04 Three days of essential presentations, performances, and debates

05 **FUSE98** is an event that will consist of presentations, installations, film and video projections, and sound performances by an eclectic array of practitioners representing the leading edge of contemporary design. Their specific charter at **FUSE98** will be to catalyst a new and vital vision of the fundamental nature of the communications world, and to inspire a renewed understanding of the technological context in which that world is embedded

06 A visual language laboratory published four times per year

07 A moving mix of sound and image, word and space

08

09 Wednesday, Thursday, Friday

PARTICIPANTS:

ANTIROM
AUDIOROM
DAVID BERLOW
NEVILLE BRODY
DAVID CARSON
MATTHEW CARTER
DAVID CROW
SASHA FRERE-JONES
TOBIAS FRERE-JONES
MALCOLM GARRETT
BILL HILL
KARRIE JACOBS
TIBOR KALMAN
JEFFERY KEEDY
SANFORD KWINTER
BRUCE MAU
REBECA MENDEZ
PANASONIC
GILES ROLLESTONE
PETER SAVILLE
ERIK SPIEKERMANN
LUCILLE TENAZAS
ALEXEI TYLEVICH
ERIK VAN BLOKLAND
JUST VAN ROSSUM
JOHN WARWICKER
CHRIS WATSON
MIKE WILLIAMS
JON WOZENCROFT
MORE TO COME

METADESIGNNEVILLEBRODYFONTSHOPINTERNATIONALPRESENT

THEVITALDESIGNEVENTOFTHEYEAR:

 FUSE98:BEYONDTYPOGRAPHY

SANFRANCISCOMAY27-291998

CORPORATE IDENTITY

. . . .

Design
Mike Abbink and John Close
San Francisco, California
. . . .

Creative Direction
Neville Brody and Rick Lowe
London, England and
San Francisco, California
. . . .

Agency
MetaDesign
. . . .

Client
Fuse Conferences
. . . .

Principal Type
Interstate
. . . .

Dimensions
Various

WEB SITE

. . . .

Design
Olivier Chetelat, Shawn
Hazen, and Eva Walter
San Francisco, California
. . . .

Creative Direction
Rick Lowe
. . . .

Producer
David Peters
. . . .

Technical Direction
Joseph Ternes
. . . .

Agency
MetaDesign
. . . .

Client
Fuse Conferences
. . . .

Principal Type
Interstate

BROCHURE

. . . .

Design
Mike Abbink
San Francisco, California
. . . .

Creative Direction
Neville Brody and Rick Lowe
London, England and
San Francisco, California
. . . .

Writers
Jon Wozencroft and
Christopher Myers
London, England and
San Francisco, California
. . . .

Agency
MetaDesign
. . . .

Client
Fuse Conferences
. . . .

Principal Type
Interstate
. . . .

Dimensions
8 x 11 in. (20.3 x 27.9 cm)

Theatre S³ presents

Edward Albee's
The American Dream

Directed and designed
by Victor D'Altorio
Assisted by
Laura Sturm
Featuring Laura Bailey,
Deborah Frieden, Harrison,
Sondra Sellars and Bill
Anthony Woods

All seats $20
Previews $15
Students, seniors and
groups of 20 or more
$17.50

Victory Gardens Theater
Downstairs Studio
2257 North Lincoln
Chicago
Previews
Thursday, July 9th
through Sunday, July 12th
Opening Night
Thursday July 16, 1998
Thursdays, Fridays and
Saturdays at 8:30 pm
Sundays at 3:30pm

For tickets
call 773/871-3000

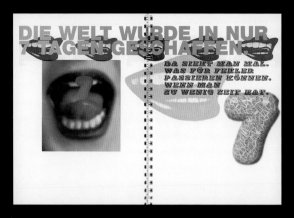

BROCHURE

Design
Joerg Bauer
Stuttgart, Germany

Lettering
Joerg Bauer

Art Direction
Joerg Bauer

Creative Direction
Joerg Bauer

Agency
Joerg Bauer Design

Client
Filderandruckstudio

Principal Type
Handel Gothic, Trade
Gothic, Suburban, Leucadia
Beached Fish, Confidential,
and Decorated 035

Dimensions
6⅛ x 8¼ in. (15.5 x 21 cm)

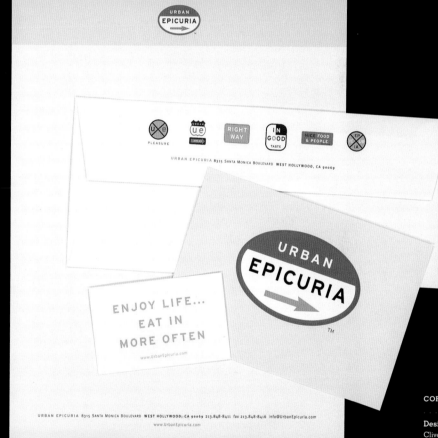

POSTER

Design
Michael Bierut
New York, New York

Lettering
Michael Bierut

Studio
Pentagram Design

Client
THEATRE S³

Principal Type
Handlettering

Dimensions
36 x 24 in. (91.4 x 61 cm)

◄

CORPORATE IDENTITY

Design
Clive Piercy
Santa Monica, California

Creative Direction
Clive Piercy and Michael
Hodgson

Design Office
Ph.D

Client
Urban Epicuria

Principal Type
Interstate, Meta, and Matrix
Script

Dimensions
Various

BROCHURE

. . . .

Design
Alisa Wolfson and Christin
Spagnoli
Chicago, Illinois

. . . .

Lettering
Christin Spagnoli

. . . .

Creative Direction
James Koval

. . . .

Design Office
VSA Partners

. . . .

Client
Howard Bjornson
Photography

. . . .

Principal Type
Baskerville

. . . .

Dimensions
8 x 10½ in. (20.3 x 26.7 cm)

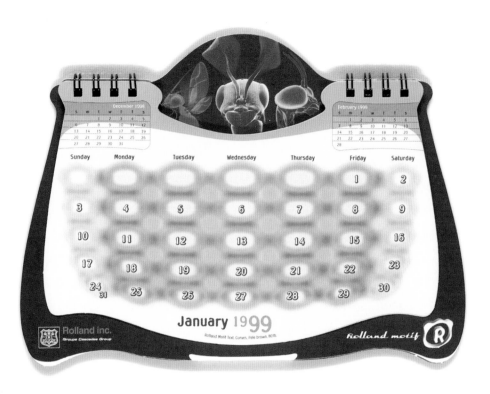

CAMPAIGN

. . . .

Design
Marc Serre, Michel Valois,
and Christine Côté
Montréal, Québec, Canada

. . . .

Art Direction
Marc Serre

. . . .

Creative Direction
Daniel Fortin, George Fok,
and Marc Serre

. . . .

Micro Photography
Dennis Kunkel and John
Tsukano
Kailua, Hawaii and
Honolulu, Hawaii

. . . .

Agency
époxy

. . . .

Client
Rolland, Inc.

. . . .

Principal Type
Oculus

. . . .

Dimensions
Various

INSTRUCTIONAL SERIES
CANINE HOUSEKEEPER

A useful guide to training your dog to do all the things you don't want to do.

Just like humans, some dogs are smarter than others. (In fact, some dogs are smarter than some humans. You can probably think of a few examples yourself.) So hang in there if your pet turns out to be some sort of canine lamebrain. Repetition will be the key to success.

TRAINING TIPS

LESSON 1: GARBAGE REMOVAL

COMMAND	ACTION
"Grab"	Instruct your canine to grab the bag at its opening to avoid a major tear.
"Carry"	Then, be sure he lifts and carries it off the ground. Don't drag the bag.
"Deposit"	Finally, it needs to go "in" the can. Not "on" it. Not "near" it. Inside it.

GOAL

If your canine just can't figure it out, try putting the bag in your mouth and demonstrating it for him. **HINT:** this is best done when no one else is watching.

1 Reward a task well done:

 A). A few of these are ample reward for first-time success.

 B). Give this tasty morsel when he consistently comes through.

 C). Lay this on him when he does a chore without being asked.

 D). Just kidding.

2 Provide frequent rest periods:

Every year of your life equals seven dog years. So your hound is working some really long hours.

Chore	Your time	In dog years
Empty garbage	4 min.	28 min.
Tidy up room	45 min.	5 hrs., 15 min.
Pulling weeds	4 hrs.	1 day, 4 hrs.

3 Relax and enjoy your new free time:

▸ Sit in the bathtub and get all wrinkly.
▸ Prove the existence of extraterrestrial life.
▸ Practice juggling corndogs.

LESSON 2: TIDYING UP

After garbage removal this should be a snap. Just be sure your pooch knows the difference between a garbage can and a clothes hamper. If not, you could end up short of underwear.

?

TRASH   HAMPER

ADVANCED LESSON: AUTO CLEANING

This should be attempted with hounds of exceptional intellect and dexterity, only. If your canine is a bit of a putz, don't even waste the time trying to teach this one.

Bonus Reward

 x2

LESSON 3: PULLING WEEDS

 Weed "YES"

 Flower "NO"

Dogs don't have a green thumb (heck, they don't have a thumb of any kind). Therefore, you need to help them distinguish between a weed and a flower. If you don't, well, let's put it this way, your mutt won't be the only one living in the proverbial doghouse.

ADVERTISEMENT

. . . .

Design
Todd Piper-Hauswirth
Minneapolis, Minnesota

. . . .

Art Direction
Charles S. Anderson and
Todd Piper-Hauswirth

. . . .

Creative Direction
Francis Timony
New York, New York

. . . .

Agency
Cliff Freeman and Partners

. . . .

Client
Cherry Coke

. . . .

Principal Type
Univers Condensed and
Trade Gothic Bold
Condensed

. . . .

Dimensions
19 x 25 in. (48.3 x 63.5 cm)

◄

POSTER AND BOOK

. . . .

Design
Hideki Nakajima
Tokyo, Japan

. . . .

Art Direction
Hideki Nakajima

. . . .

Creative Direction
Shigeki Yamakado

. . . .

Photography
Various

. . . .

Agency
Shigoto-Ba, Inc. and Dentsu

. . . .

Studio
Nakajima Design

. . . .

Client
Seiko

. . . .

Principal Type
Custom type

. . . .

Dimensions
Various

Design
Lyle Owerko
New York, New York

Art Direction
Lyle Owerko

Creative Direction
Lyle Owerko

Photography
Lyle Owerko

Agency
Compound

Principal Type
Frutiger

Dimensions
10½ x 8 in. (26.7 x 20.3 cm)

compound

Creative Direction
Andreas Uebele
Stuttgart, Germany

Illustration
Oliver Sorg

Studio
Büro Uebele Visuelle
Kommunikation

Client
Sorg et Frosch Planungs
GmbH, Architekten

Principal Type
Linotype Univers 130, 230,
330, 430, and 530

Dimensions
6½ x 4¾ in. (16.5 x 12 cm)

---

subcultures are (re)appropriating from the environment

(The present contains nothing more than the past, and what is found in the effect was already in the cause.)
- Henri L. Bergson.

Our era is seeing the breakdown of the barrier between the organic and inorganic. There is a merging equation of ideas and matter that exists beyond the epistemological that goes further than combinatorics to understand creativity. Henry David Thoreau wrote of "the pattern which connects" in his ruminations regarding Walden Pond. If a "connective pattern" exists between all things (animate and inanimate) how could we best describe creative evolution?

[The] veil between the organic and the manufactured has crumpled to reveal that the two really are, and have always been, of one being.
- Kevin Kelly, Out of Control.

Kevin Lyons in his article Cease and Desist (AIGA Journal Vol 14 No#1) writes that, "...by appropriating old symbols and images, we are in effect paying homage to the originals—a form of cultural archaeology. We reformulate, change the context and make kids recognize and rethink logos and images. The mere reappropriated symbols take on new cultural identities." The sentiment of current street culture dictates that if something is in your face you have a right to reference it. In doing so you are honoring it by passing its "genetic material" on to new entities. It's not stealing. It's evolution. William J. Mitchell's book, The Reconfigured Eye — Visual Truth in the Post Photographic Era examines many sides to this issue. Mitchell states that, "We must abandon the traditional conception of an art world populated by stable, enduring, finished works and replace it with one that recognizes continual mutation and proliferation of variants—much as with oral epic poetry."

Regarding the tangled subjectivity of oneself and the dated conventions in the era of communication, Douglas Rushkoff states, "The increasing non-linearity of our media and popular culture is not a heathen retreat from the dualistic morality of God, but the process by which we learn to accept the very natural, even organic quality of complexity, interrelatedness, and a property of life called chaos." Inextricably bound to data input, individual belief structures form around patterns perceived from the incessant stream of media images and icons.

Where there is truth there is chaos. Where there is chaos there is truth.

data chaos is the media climate

The atomization of media society fueled by the cult of
the individual perspective is providing a new radical-   (Quanta)
ized world perspective. The autonomous as subject is
being pushed to an extreme. Media-icons are birthing
a culture of the hieroglyphic. Industrialization is the
triumph of the chaotic phenomenon of allurement
and mass production. What is possible becomes reality. What becomes reality is manipulatable. The variant between sign and signification is an evolving shifting paradigm. Writing in Adweek ("The End is the Beginning" September 23, 1996) Barbara Lippert observes that, "Other media and art forms are getting more like advertising, and not the other way around. The reductive message, the skillful isolation of the moment, the visual manipulation and seduction, the endless repetition—that's the future, for better or worse." Techno-civilization communicates through the metaphorical language of (re)configured signs. The fetishized character of objects becomes "The Real Thing" as legitimate as the original. Ultimately, metaphors have become the language of chaos.

variation

change

("truth" and "origin" are no longer valid categories of judgement)

constitutive

productive

difference

Brillo

Brillo
10
steel wool soap pads
long lasting resists rust
tough cleaning brilliant shine

1.1 Stainless steel rods

Our rosso curtain rods offer almost unlimited
possibilities. Ceiling mounting or wall mounting.
Vertical or horizontal. The ends of the rods are f
allowing different endpieces (finials) to be adde
We can also bend the rods according to your
template or dimensions. Special dimensions are
also no problem. We cut rods and brackets to yo
requirements with speed and precision.

Double-run brackets are available for double
runs. Here, too, special dimensions are no proble
Our intermediate brackets allow support of long
rods without hindering pulling of the curtain (cl
run). (Matching accessories: Curtain rings for cl
run).

Two types of corner connector are available:
screw-in and plug-in. Special brackets are also
available. Please send details for corner bracket
by faxing us a dimensional drawing. Use
wallmounts for alcove mounting.

The patented clamping ring ensures maximur
freedom for fastening the fabric, whether sewn
not, with or without tape, eyelets, thimbles etc.
Posters, sketches and plans can also be held wit
the clamping ring. Steel or gathering hooks are
used for conventional fastening.

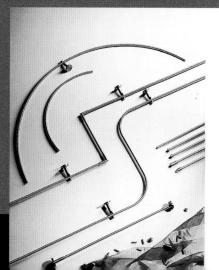

tweeduizend two thousand -1

DIARY
. . . .

Design
Hans Bockting, Will
de l'Ecluse, Julius van der
Woude, and Nick Bell
Amsterdam, The Netherlands
and London, England
. . . .

Creative Direction
Hans Bockting and Will
de l'Ecluse
. . . .

Typography
Will de l'Ecluse and Julius
van der Woude
. . . .

Design Office
UNA (Amsterdam/London)
designers
. . . .

Client
UNA, Colorset, Haskerland,
and Veenman
. . . .

Principal Type
Akzidenz Grotesk
. . . .

Dimensions
8⅝ x 10 in. (22.5 x 25.5 cm)

fall 1 | women | intimate | girls

men | boys | fall 1

autumn harvest colors

CAMPAIGN

Design
Sharon Werner, Sarah
Nelson, and Elizabeth
McKinnell
Minneapolis, Minnesota

Art Direction
Sharon Werner

Studio
Werner Design Werks, Inc.

Client
Target Stores/Trend
Department

KIT

. . . .

Design
Claude Skelton
Baltimore, Maryland

. . . .

Art Direction
Claude Skelton

. . . .

Creative Direction
Claude Skelton

. . . .

Photography
Peter Howard

. . . .

Agency
Claude Skelton Design and
Neustadt Creative Marketing

. . . .

Client
St. John's College

. . . .

Principal Type
ITC Bodoni

. . . .

Dimensions
7 x 10 in. (17.8 x 25.4 cm)

{ TO THE READER }

St. John's College believes that the way to a liberal education lies through a direct and sustained engagement with the books in which the greatest minds of our civilization have expressed themselves. To that end, the college offers a four-year nonelective program in which students read, discuss, and write about the seminal works that have shaped the world in which we live. § There is no other college quite like St. John's. Here, there are no lecture courses, no textbooks, no written finals, no departments, no research professors. Instead, the college offers small discussion classes, books that are classics, oral examinations at the end of each semester, a single ☞

ST JOHN'S College

ANNAPOLIS · SANTA FE

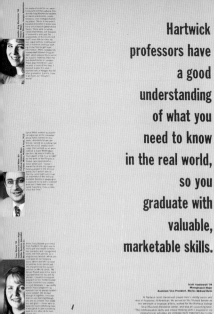

Hartwick professors have a good understanding of what you need to know in the real world, so you graduate with valuable, marketable skills.

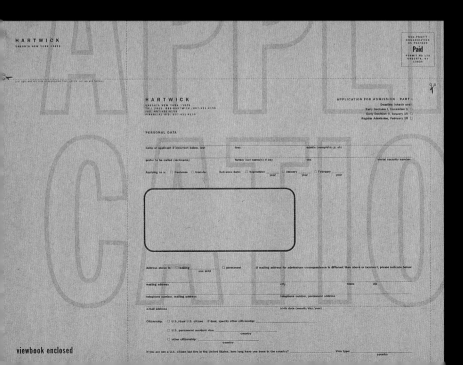

viewbook enclosed

BROCHURE

Design
Priscilla Henderer
Baltimore, Maryland

Art Direction
Anthony Rutka and Priscilla
Henderer

Illustration
David Butler and Jeffrey
Fisher
Mount Vernon, Ohio and
New York, New York

Design Studio
Rutka Weadock Design

Client
Hartwick College

Principal Type
Franklin Gothic

Dimensions
11 x 17 in. (27.9 x 43.2 cm)

TV OPENING

. . . .

Design

Greg Hahn

New York, New York

. . . .

Art Direction

Greg Hahn and Todd
St. John

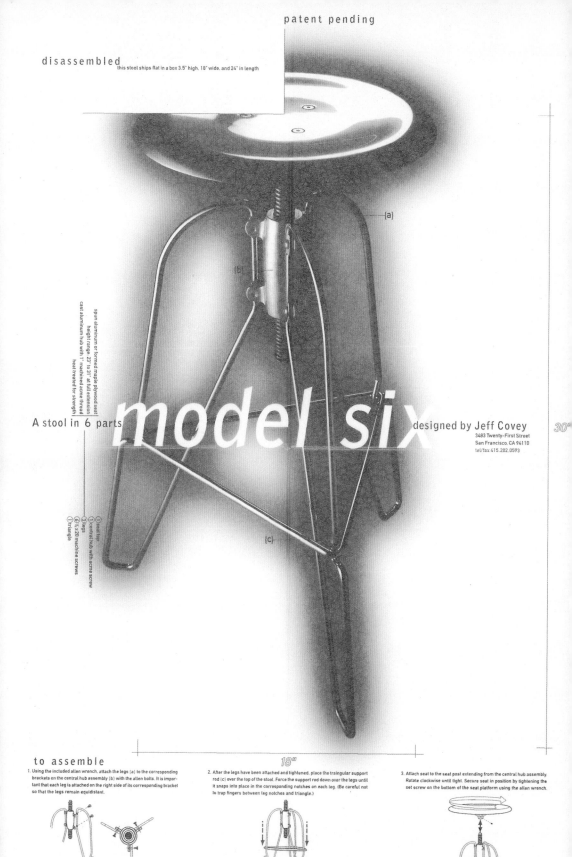

patent pending

disassembled
this stool ships flat in a box 3.5" high, 18" wide, and 24" in length

(a)

(b)

spun aluminum or formed maple plywood seat
height range: 23" to 31" at full extension
cast aluminum hub with 1" machined acme thread
heat treated for strength

A stool in 6 parts *model six* designed by **Jeff Covey**
3483 Twenty-First Street
San Francisco, CA 94110
tel/fax 415.282.0593

30"

(c)

1 seat top
1 central hub with acme screw
3 legs
6 ¼ x 20 machine screws
1 triangle

18"

to assemble

1. Using the included allen wrench, attach the legs (a) to the corresponding brackets on the central hub assembly (b) with the allen bolts. It is important that each leg is attached on the right side of its corresponding bracket so that the legs remain equidistant.

2. After the legs have been attached and tightened, place the traingular support rod (c) over the top of the stool. Force the support rod down over the legs until it snaps into place in the corresponding notches on each leg. (Be careful not to trap fingers between leg notches and triangle.)

3. Attach seat to the seat post extending from the central hub assembly. Rotate clockwise until tight. Secure seat in position by tightening the set screw on the bottom of the seat platform using the allen wrench.

POSTER

. . . .

Design
Jeremy Mende and Raul
Cabra
San Francisco, California

. . . .

Art Direction
Raul Cabra

. . . .

Photography
Matt Farruggio

. . . .

Design Office
Cabra Diseño

. . . .

Client
Jeff Covey

. . . .

Principal Type
News Gothic and Bell
Gothic

. . . .

Dimensions
16 x 24 in. (40.6 x 61 cm)

CATALOG

. . . .

Design
David Bates and Lisa
Cerveny
Seattle, Washington

. . . .

Art Direction
Jack Anderson and David
Bates

. . . .

Photography
Condit Studios

. . . .

Illustration
Jack Unruh

. . . .

Studio
Hornall Anderson Design
Works, Inc.

. . . .

Client
Leatherman Tool Group

. . . .

Principal Type
Bell Gothic

. . . .

Dimensions
6 x 11 in. (15.2 x 27.9 cm)

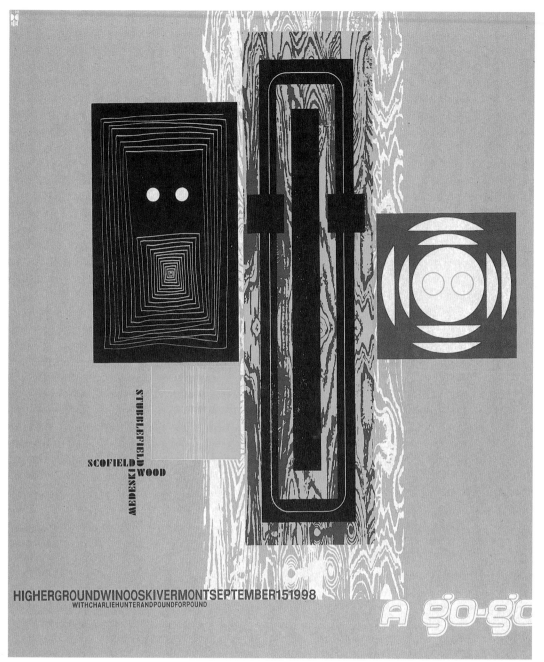

POSTER

Design
David Covell
Burlington, Vermont

Art Direction
David Covell

Creative Direction
Michael Jager

Studio
Jager Di Paola Kemp Design

Client
Higher Ground

Principal Type
Roland, Futura Black, and
Trade Gothic

Dimensions
22 x 26⅛ in. (55.9 x
66.4 cm)

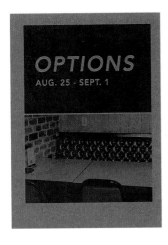

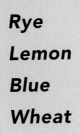

OPTIONS
AUG. 25 - SEPT. 1

Rye
Lemon
Blue
Wheat

Trap
Paper
Storm
Bar

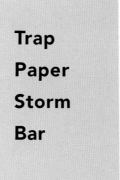

BROCHURE

. . . .

Design
Bob Dinetz and Kevin Roberson
San Francisco, California

. . . .

Art Direction
Bill Cahan

. . . .

Creative Direction
Bill Cahan

. . . .

Agency
Cahan & Associates

. . . .

Client
Mohawk Paper Mills, Inc.

. . . .

Principal Type
Avenir

. . . .

Dimensions
8¼ x 10½ in. (21 x 26.7 cm)

BROCHURE

Design
Sharon Werner and Sarah
Nelson
Minneapolis, Minnesota

Lettering
Elvis Swift
Naples, Florida

Art Direction
Sharon Werner

Illustration
Elvis Swift

Printer
Nomadic Press
St. Paul, Minnesota

Studio
Werner Design Werks, Inc.

Client
Joanie Bernstein, Art Rep
and Elvis Swift

Principal Type
Trixie, Minion, and
handlettering

Dimensions
7 x 9½ in. (17.8 x 24.1 cm)

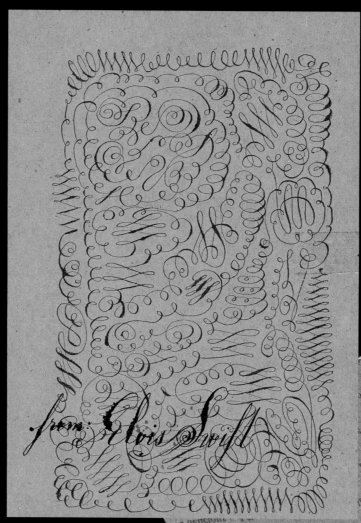

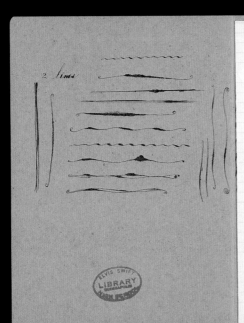

Bob

This is Bob.
He built and ran billion-dollar
businesses at IBM.

They
all
quit.

BROCHURE
. . . .
Design
John Bielenberg and
Erik Cox
San Francisco, California
. . . .
Creative Direction
John Bielenberg
. . . .
Writer
Rich Binell
San Jose, California
. . . .
Design Office
Bielenberg Design
. . . .
Client
Scient
. . . .
Principal Type
Frutiger
. . . .
Dimensions
8½ x 10 in. (21.6 x 25.4 cm)

Because they are not
content to do business
the old way.

Because they
are not content to sit
and stagnate.

And because they
are convinced that the
electronic business
revolution is the greatest
opportunity in history.

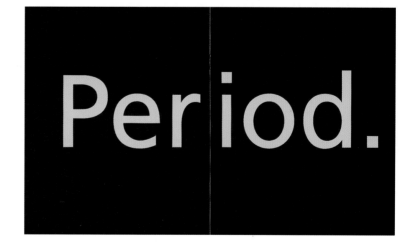

Period.

COR THERAPEUTICS, INC.
1997 Annual Report

ANNUAL REPORT

. . . .

Design
Michael Braley
San Francisco, California

. . . .

Art Direction
Bill Cahan

. . . .

Creative Direction
Bill Cahan

. . . .

Agency
Cahan & Associates

. . . .

Client
COR Therapeutics, Inc.

. . . .

Principal Type
Trade Gothic

. . . .

Dimensions
9⅝ x 11⅞ in. (24.4 x
30.2 cm)

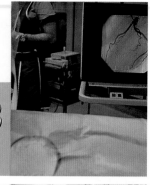

CATH LAB

ER

Over 1.5 million people in the U.S. will have heart attacks this year, and 500,000 of them will die.

"We have an 80-year-old male in 'step down' this morning, with a 2-week history of chest pain that resolves with rest. He upped his anti-anginal medication himself and is pain-free now, but he called us and thought he should come in."

"A 43-year-old white male with hypertension and kidney disease had intermittent pain on exertion, and recently more severe radiating pain several days ago. They wanted us to take a look at him."

ECHO

An echocardiogram, or "echo," is a non-invasive way of determining heart function using ultrasound. It can detect whether a patient has a malfunctioning valve, or a wall-motion abnormality that might indicate that an MI has occurred. Doctors can also monitor patients with congestive heart failure using echocardiography to determine how blood flows through the heart and the volume of the ejection fraction being pumped from the heart. And of course echocardiograms can help cardiologists to assess the success or failure of bypass surgery. Although echocardiograms can image all four chambers of the heart, the health of the muscle, and the volume of blood flow, the one thing "echos" can't do is look at the vasculature of the heart. That is the province of the invasive cardiac catheterization procedure.

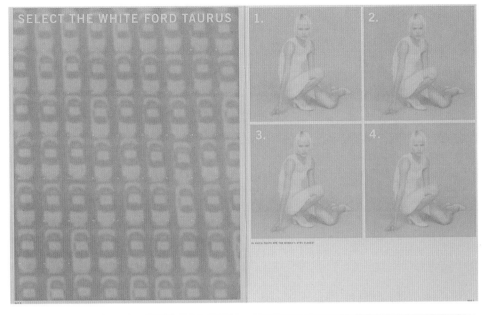

SELECT THE WHITE FORD TAURUS

1. 2. 3. 4.

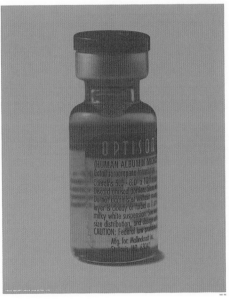

WELCOME TO THE NEW AGE OF ULTRASOUND IMAGING. DEVELOPED BY MOLECULAR BIOSYSTEMS, OPTISON™ CONTRAST ECHO HELPS CARDIOLOGISTS DIAGNOSE WITH CONFIDENCE. NO MORE FUZZ-O-GRAMS.

OPTISON
(HUMAN ALBUMIN

BROCHURE

. . . .

Design
Jason Schulte and Erik Johnson
Minneapolis, Minnesota

. . . .

Art Direction
Charles S. Anderson

. . . .

Copywriter
P. J. Chmiel

. . . .

Studio
Charles S. Anderson Design

. . . .

Client
French Paper Company

. . . .

Principal Type
Trade Gothic Extended

. . . .

Dimensions
11 x 17 in. (27.9 x 43.2 cm)

ANNUAL REPORT

. . . .

Design
Kevin Roberson
San Francisco, California

. . . .

Art Direction
Bill Cahan

. . . .

Creative Direction
Bill Cahan

. . . .

Agency
Cahan & Associates

. . . .

Client
Molecular Biosystems, Inc.

. . . .

Principal Type
Trade Gothic

. . . .

Dimensions
10 x 12½ in. (25.4 x 31.8 cm)

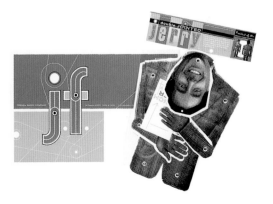

Himmelslichter
Chor und Orgel · 's Rankler Chörle

PACKAGING

Design
Peter Felder
Rankweil, Austria

Lettering
Peter Felder

Art Direction
Peter Felder

Printer
Johannes Thurnher

Design Office
Felder Grafikdesign

Client
's Rankler Chörle + Gebhard
Mathis

Principal Type
Minion and Trajan

Dimensions
4¾ x 4¾ in. (12 x 12 cm)

TV COMMERCIAL

Design
Eric Smith and Eric Cruz
Los Angeles, California

Art Direction
Michael Riley

Creative Direction
Peter Frankfurt

Producer
Saffron Kenny

Studio
Imaginary Forces

Client
The Jun Group

Principal Type
Cruz Bold

Boek x

lelies, geverfde knikkers, barnsteenkralen – tranen van
de Heliadenbomen –, daarna tooit hij haar met kleren,
doet ringen aan haar vingers, lange snoeren om haar hals,
haar oren krijgen lichte parelhangers, ook haar borsten
zijn rijk behangen. Alles siert haar, ook al is zij mooi
zonder dat al. Hij legt haar op een roodgespreide divan,
noemt haar zijn bedvriendin en doet haar zachtjes met haar hals
in veren kussens leunen, denkend dat zij dat kan voelen!

250   Het feest van Venus, overal op Cyprus hoogtijdag,
was aangebroken. Jonge koeien met vergulde horens
vielen ten offer aan de slagen in hun blanke nek
en wierook geurde op. Pygmalion bleef na het offer
bij 't altaar staan en sprak een stille wens: "O goden, als
u alles geven kunt, geef mij een vrouw..." – hij had de moed niet
"die van ivoor" te zeggen, wel "die lijkt op mijn ivoren..."
De gouden Venus, zelf aanwezig bij haar feest, begreep
wat deze wens beduidde: driemaal schoot de vlam hoog op
en blies een vuurtong in de lucht, ten teken van genade.

280   Zodra hij thuiskomt, haast hij zich naar zijn geliefde beeld,
nestelt zich naast haar, kust haar mond. Zij lijkt erdoor te smelten,
hij kust haar weer, raakt met een vingertop haar borsten aan:
het aangeraakt ivoor wordt week, de kilte lijkt verdwenen,
het voegt zich naar zijn druk, is soepel, zoals bijenwas
van de Hymettus zacht wordt door de zon en zich laat drukken
tot vele vormen en juist door het kneden kneedbaar wordt.
Terwijl hij eerst verbijsterd nog geen vreugde toelaat, bang voor
bedrog, streelt hij verliefd steeds weer, steeds meer dat lieve beeld
en streelt een vrouw: zijn tasten doet haar bloed veel sneller stromen!

290   Dan spreekt Pygmalion, de held van Paphos, woorden uit
waarmee hij Venus dankt, diep uit zijn hart, en drukt zijn lippen

18

BROCHURE

. . . .

Design
Hans Bockting, Will
de l'Ecluse, and Alain
Soetermans
Amsterdam, The Netherlands

. . . .

Creative Direction
Hans Bockting

. . . .

Typographer
Will de l'Ecluse

. . . .

Design Office
UNA (Amsterdam) designers

. . . .

Client
TreBruk Benelux, Belgium

. . . .

Principal Type
Trinité

. . . .

Dimensions
6½ x 8⅞ in. (16.5 x 22.5 cm)

STATIONERY

. . . .

Design
Jennifer Wyville
Chicago, Illinois

. . . .

Lettering
Jennifer Wyville

. . . .

Design Office
Wyville, USA

. . . .

Client
Kaye Harrell

. . . .

Principal Type
Mrs. Eaves and Bickman

. . . .

Dimensions
2 x 3½ in. (5.1 x 8.9 cm)

T-SHIRT

. . . .

Design
Ted Skibinski and Jim Keller
Ithaca, New York

. . . .

Agency
Iron Design

. . . .

Principal Type
Trade Gothic Condensed
and Century Schoolbook
Bold Italic

Design
Rita Marshall
Lakeville, Connecticut

Art Direction
Rita Marshall

Studio
Delessert and Marshall

Principal Type
Berthold Bodoni

Dimensions
8½ x 11 in. (21.6 x 27.9 cm)

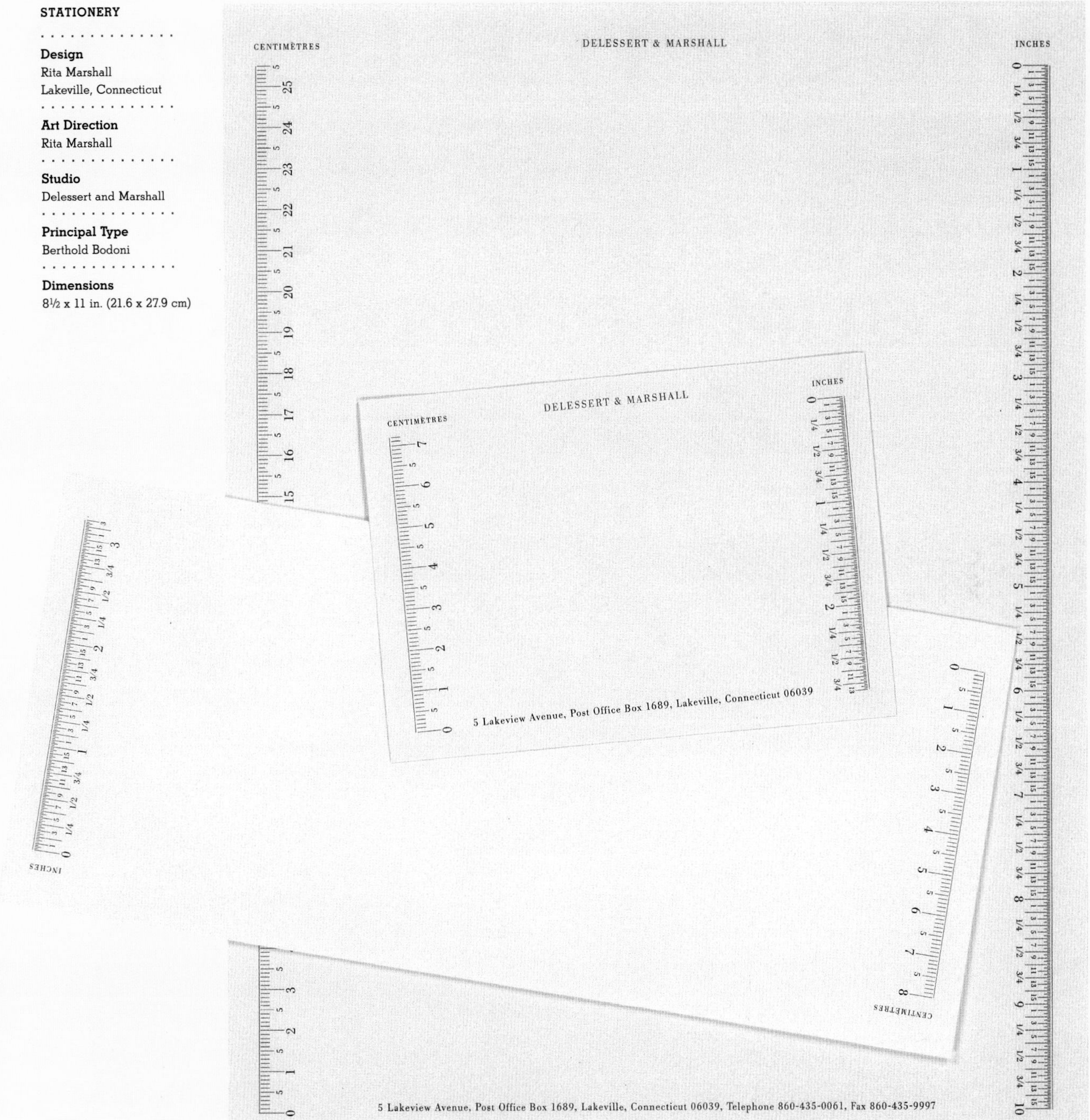

DELESSERT & MARSHALL

DELESSERT & MARSHALL

5 Lakeview Avenue, Post Office Box 1689, Lakeville, Connecticut 06039

5 Lakeview Avenue, Post Office Box 1689, Lakeville, Connecticut 06039, Telephone 860-435-0061, Fax 860-435-9997

MY LITTLE LOVER
SPECIAL ISSUE #2
"The Waters" 12.3 OUT
ALBUM + PHOTO BOOK

PHOTOGRAPHER HIROSHI NOMURA, ART DIRECTOR TOSHIAKI UCHIKOSHI, PRODUCED BY TAKESHI KOBAYASHI

LIVE REMIX VIDEO
"SIGN OF THURSDAY" 12.3 OUT

1997. 11. 20 (THURS) AT LIQUID ROOM

VISUAL DIRECTOR SHUUICHI TAN

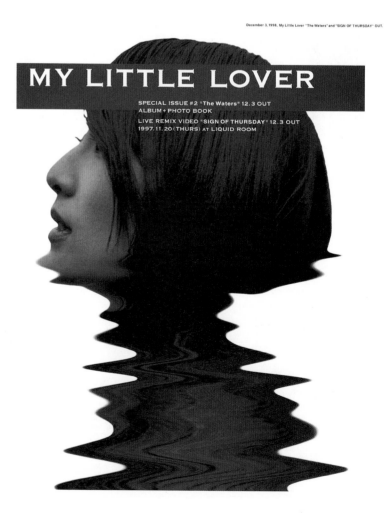

December 3, 1998, My Little Lover "The Waters" and "SIGN OF THURSDAY" OUT.

MY LITTLE LOVER

SPECIAL ISSUE #2 "The Waters" 12.3 OUT
ALBUM + PHOTO BOOK

LIVE REMIX VIDEO "SIGN OF THURSDAY" 12.3 OUT
1997. 11. 20 (THURS) AT LIQUID ROOM

MAGAZINE

· · · · · · · · · · · · ·

Design
Eiji Yamada, Naoko Nodera,
and Kiyoshi Tsukamoto
Tokyo, Japan

· · · · · · · · · · · · ·

Art Direction
Eiji Yamada

· · · · · · · · · · · · ·

Creative Direction
Hidetoshi Kimura and Moto
Takagi

· · · · · · · · · · · · ·

Agency
Dentsu, Inc.

· · · · · · · · · · · · ·

Design Office
Ultra Graphics

· · · · · · · · · · · · ·

Client
Toys Factory

· · · · · · · · · · · · ·

Principal Type
Copperplate

· · · · · · · · · · · · ·

Dimensions
11^{7}/16 x 13^{11}/16 in. (29 x
35 cm)

BOOK

. . . .

Design

Michelle Benzer, Michael
Carabetta, Sarah Crumb,
Patricia Evangelista, Julia
Flagg, Pamela Geismar,
Carole Goodman, Kristin
Holder, Natalie Johnstone,
Sing Lin, Laura Lovett,
Sushma Patel, Liz Rico, Toby
Salk, Joseph Stitzlein,
Martine Trélaün, and Nina
Turner
San Francisco, California

. . . .

Art Direction

Pamela Geismar

. . . .

Client

Chronicle Books

. . . .

Principal Type

Bodoni, Helvetica, Times
Roman, Century, and Futura

. . . .

Dimensions

5½ x 6 in. (14 x 15 cm)

IT ISN'T A
QUESTION OF
ENHANCEMENT
THROUGH DESIGN.
WHETHER AN
EDITOR REALIZES
IT OR NOT, DESIGN
IS PART OF WHAT
HE DOES EVERY
TIME HE PRINTS
THE PAPER. —
LOUIS SILVERSTEIN

PACKAGING
. . . .

Design
Chris Bilheimer, Michael
Stipe, and Brook Dillon
Athens, Georgia
. . . .

Art Direction
Chris Bilheimer, Michael
Stipe, and Brook Dillon
. . . .

Photography
Emer Patten and Nick
Wickham
. . . .

Client
Warner Bros. Records
. . . .

Principal Type
Courier and Compacta Bold
. . . .

Dimensions
4¾ x 4¾ in. (12.1 x 12.1 cm)

CORPORATE IDENTITY
. . . .

Design
Fons M. Hickmann and
Gesine Grotrian-Steinweg
Düsseldorf, Germany
. . . .

Art Direction
Gesine Grotrian-Steinweg
and Fons M. Hickmann
. . . .

Editor
Nicolai Sokolow
. . . .

Studio
Hickmann-Grotrian
. . . .

Client
escale
. . . .

Principal Type
Corporate
. . . .

Dimensions
Various

. . . .

Design
Clive Piercy
Santa Monica, California

. . . .

Creative Direction
Clive Piercy and Michael
Hodgson

. . . .

Design Office
Ph.D

. . . .

Client
Chemistry

. . . .

Principal Type
Meta and Interstate

. . . .

Dimensions
Various

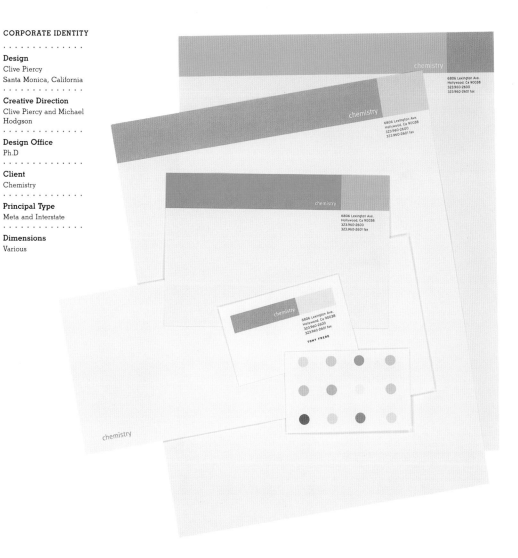

Der Sturm des Herbstes
Zerrupft dem Teufelsauge
Die roten Blüten.
Issa (1763-1827)

BROCHURE

. . . .

Art Direction
Josephine Prokop and
Jochen Theurer
Düsseldorf and Frankfurt,
Germany

. . . .

Creative Direction
Claus Koch and Josephine
Prokop

. . . .

Agency
Claus Koch Corporate
Communications GmbH

. . . .

Principal Type
Polo Light and Polo Semi
Bold

. . . .

Dimensions
5⁷/₈ x 8¹/₄ in. (14.8 x 21 cm)

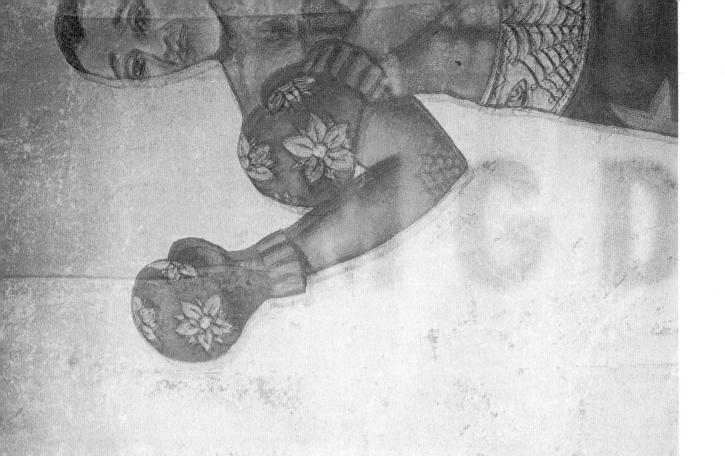

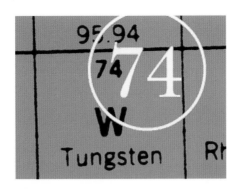

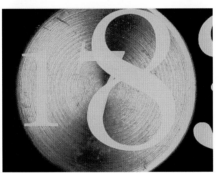

STUDENT WORK
. . . .

Design
Matthew Tragesser
Pittsburgh, Pennsylvania
. . . .

School
Carnegie Mellon University
. . . .

Instructor
Dan Boyarski
. . . .

Principal Type
FF Letter Gothic Text and
ITC New Baskerville

POSTER
. . . .

Design
Hal Wolverton and Joe Peila
Portland, Oregon
. . . .

Lettering
Hal Wolverton, Heath Lowe,
Joe Peila, Sarah Starr, Alan
Foster, Neil Gust, Mary
Kysar, and Topher Sinkinson
. . . .

Art Direction
Hal Wolverton
. . . .

Creative Direction
Alicia Johnson and Hal
Wolverton
. . . .

Photography
Melody McDaniel
Los Angeles, California
. . . .

Illustration
Rob and Christian Clayton
Los Angeles, California
. . . .

Agency
Wieden & Kennedy
. . . .

Studio
Johnson & Wolverton
. . . .

Client
Miller Brewing Co.
. . . .

Principal Type
Interstate (modified)
. . . .

Dimensions
20 x 30 in. (50.8 x 76.2 cm)

Creative Direction
Professor Volker Liesfeld

Photography
Simone Schmitt and Jan
Steinhilber

School
Fachhochschule Wiesbaden

Principal Type
Caecilia

BROCHURE

. . . .

Design
Will de l'Ecluse and Mark
Diaper
Amsterdam, The Netherlands
. . . .

Creative Direction
Will de l'Ecluse
. . . .

Typographer
Will de l'Ecluse
. . . .

Design Office
UNA (Amsterdam) designers,
The Netherlands
. . . .

Client
UNA (Amsterdam) designers
and Bell typo/graphic
design, London
. . . .

Principal Type
Akzidenz Grotesk
. . . .

Dimensions
5½ x 7 in. (14 x 18 cm)

POSTER

. . . .
Design
Sean Adams and Noreen
Morioka
Beverly Hills, California
. . . .
Creative Direction
Sean Adams
. . . .
Studio
AdamsMorioka
. . . .
Client
UCLA Extension
. . . .
Principal Type
Monotype Grotesque
Condensed
. . . .
Dimensions
24 x 36 in. (61 x 91.4 cm)

CAMPAIGN

. . . .
Design
Helmut Himmler
Frankfurt, Germany
. . . .
Lettering
Judith Treder
. . . .
Art Direction
Helmut Himmler
. . . .
Creative Direction
Christoph Barth and
Stefan Karl
. . . .
Copywriter
Dirk Galia
. . . .
Agency
Michael Conrad & Leo
Burnett GmbH
. . . .
Client
Galileo Deutschland GmbH
. . . .
Principal Type
Franklin Gothic Extra
Condensed, Brush Script, Du
Mathieu, Snyder Speed,
Mercurius Script, Univers
Ultra Condensed, ITC
Quorum, Reporter Two, and
Compacta BT Black
. . . .
Dimensions
Various

WENN QUÄLENDE FRAGEN IHR UNWESEN TREIBEN
Labiles System?
Drohende Abstürze?
Rabenschwarze Terminals?
Der helle Wahnsinn?
DER EWIGE HÖLLENTRIP
Es gibt einen Ausweg:
Tel. 069/22 73 67-0
Fax 069/23 75 13
GALILEO
DEUTSCHLAND
SYSTEMATISCH ANDERS

SEX CAN BE SUMMED
UP IN 3 P's:
PROCREATION, PLEASURE AND PRIDE.

POLACOLOR 59

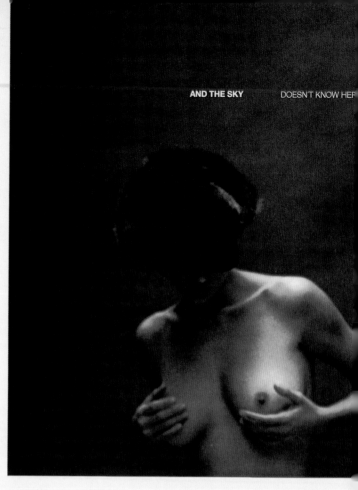

AND THE SKY   DOESN'T KNOW HER

horst

photographer

TRANSIE
NUMBER T

Horst Stasny, Los Angeles: Ph. + 1-818-760.0491, Fax + 1-818-760.8379, Zürich: Ph. +41-1-368.3355, Fax +41-1-368.3356
Austria: Ph. +43-7242-44782, Fax +43-7242-44107, e-mail: stasny@compuserve.com

BUT
IF YOU'D TRY THIS…

POLACOLOR 59

AND THE SKY   DOESN'T KNOW HE

POSTER

. . . .

Design
Horst Stasny
Thalheim bei Wels, Austria
. . . .

Art Direction
Sigi Mayer
Linz, Austria
. . . .

Creative Direction
Sigi Mayer
. . . .

Photography
Horst Stasny
. . . .

Agency
Sigi Mayer
. . . .

Client
Horst Stasny
. . . .

Principal Type
Helvetica Condensed
. . . .

Dimensions
16½ x 21 in. (41.9 x 53.3 cm)

◄

CORPORATE IDENTITY

. . . .

Design
Kerrie Powell
London, England
. . . .

Art Direction
John Rushworth
. . . .

Creative Direction
John Rushworth
. . . .

Studio
Pentagram Design Ltd.
. . . .

Client
Raffles International and
1837 Restaurant at Brown's
Hotel
. . . .

Principal Type
ITC Didi
. . . .

Dimensions
Various

PACKAGING
. . . .

Design
Sharon Werner and Sarah
Nelson
Minneapolis, Minnesota
. . . .

Calligraphy
Elvis Swift
Naples, Florida
. . . .

Art Direction
Sharon Werner
. . . .

Studio
Werner Design Werks, Inc.
. . . .

Client
Rafiki Wine Company
. . . .

Principal Type
Trixie and Minion
. . . .

Dimensions
3¼ x 2 in. (8.3 x 5.1 cm)

POSTER
. . . .

Design
Charles S. Anderson
Minneapolis, Minnesota
. . . .

Art Direction
Charles S. Anderson
. . . .

Studio
Charles S. Anderson Design
Company
. . . .

Client
Philadelphia Art Directors
Club
. . . .

Principal Type
Helvetica and found type
. . . .

Dimensions
24 x 33¾ in. (61 x 85.7 cm

WiT

WRITTEN BY
MARGARET EDSON

STAGE II
OCT 31-NOV 30
DIRECTED BY **DEREK ANSON JONES**
ARTISTIC DIRECTOR **DOUG HUGHES**
TICKETS (203) 787-4282

LONG WHARF THEATRE

Roxy Mofitt
New Haven, Connecticut

Studio
Modern Dog

Client
Long Wharf Theatre

Principal Type
Handlettering

Dimensions
18½ x 26 in. (47 x 66 cm)

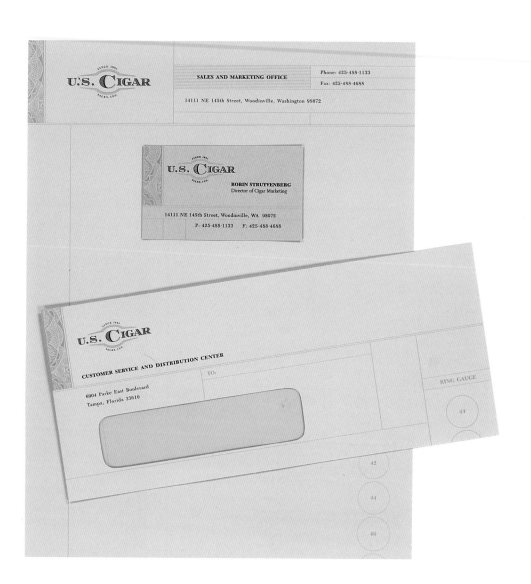

STATIONERY
. . . .
Design
Larry Anderson, Mary
Hermes, Mike Calkins, and
Michael Brugman
Seattle, Washington
. . . .
Art Direction
Jack Anderson and Larry
Anderson
. . . .
Studio
Hornall Anderson Design
Works, Inc.
. . . .
Client
U.S. Cigar
. . . .
Principal Type
Chevalier (modified) and
New Caledonia
. . . .
Dimensions
8½ x 11 in. (21.6 x 27.9 cm)

GIFT CERTIFICATE
. . . .
Design
Ed Brogna and Jim Datz
Philadelphia, Pennsylvania
. . . .
Art Direction
Ed Brogna
. . . .
Agency
Urban Outfitters
. . . .
Client
Urban Outfitters UK
. . . .
Principal Type
Vineta Ornamental and
Proxima Sans
. . . .
Dimensions
Various

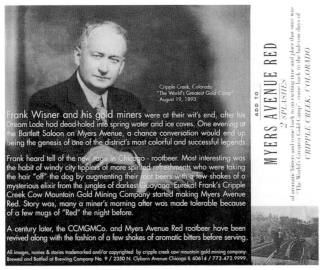

PACKAGING

· · · · · · · · · · · · ·

Design
Jennifer Wyville and B. J.
Moore
Chicago, Illinois
· · · · · · · · · · · · ·

Lettering
Jennifer Wyville
· · · · · · · · · · · · ·

Design Office
Wyville, USA
· · · · · · · · · · · · ·

Client
Cripple Creek Cow
Mountain Gold Mining Co.
· · · · · · · · · · · · ·

Principal Type
Futura, Opti-Morgan, and
Latin Condensed
· · · · · · · · · · · · ·

Dimensions
3¼ x 7½ in. (8.3 x 19.1 cm)

INTER MEDIUM INSTITUTE GRADUATE SCHOOL DTP COURSE 展 EXHIBITION • FEBRUARY 16-27 1998 • PAPER VOICE

STATIONERY

. . . .

Design
David Schrimpf
Minneapolis, Minnesota

. . . .

Creative Direction
Bill Thorburn

. . . .

Computer Artist
Phil Kjelland

. . . .

Agency
Carmichael Lynch Thorburn

. . . .

Client
Scott Companies

. . . .

Principal Type
Cheltenham

. . . .

Dimensions
8½ x 11 in. (21.6 x 27.9 cm)

▶

POSTER

. . . .

Design
Aki Inoue and Sotatsu
Tokuoka
Osaka, Japan

. . . .

Art Direction
Akio Okumura

. . . .

Studio
Packaging Create, Inc.

. . . .

Client
Inter Medium Institute
Graduate School

. . . .

Principal Type
Univers Light and custom
type

. . . .

Dimensions
28¹¹/₁₆ x 40⁹/₁₆ in. (72.8 x
103 cm)

TV COMMERCIAL

. . . .

Design
Mark Newgarden and House
Industries
Brooklyn, New York and
Wilmington, Delaware

. . . .

Lettering
Mark Newgarden

. . . .

Art Direction
Jim Spegman and Matthew
Duntemann
New York, New York

. . . .

Creative Direction
Tom Hill

. . . .

Animation
Eric Rosner

. . . .

Client
TV Land

. . . .

Principal Type
Cooper Black, Akzidenz
Grotesk Medium, Futura
Book, and Futura Medium

POSTER

. . . .

Design
Charles S. Anderson and
Zack Custer
Minneapolis, Minnesota

. . . .

Art Direction
Charles S. Anderson

. . . .

Studio
Charles S. Anderson Design
Company

. . . .

Client
Entertainment Weekly

. . . .

Principal Type
Egyptian Wide, Old Gothic
Bold, Franklin Gothic, and
found type

. . . .

Dimensions
19 x 25 in. (48.3 x 63.5 cm)

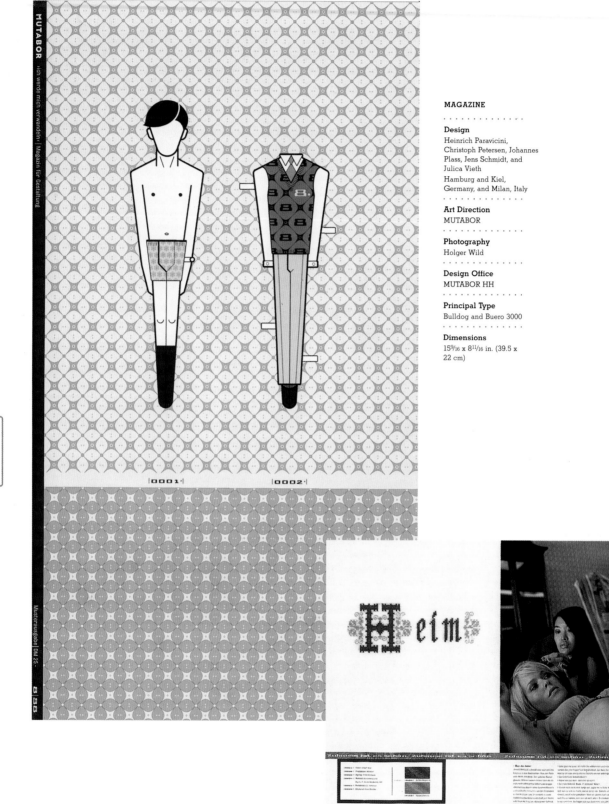

MAGAZINE

Design
Heinrich Paravicini,
Christoph Petersen, Johannes
Plass, Jens Schmidt, and
Julica Vieth
Hamburg and Kiel,
Germany, and Milan, Italy

Art Direction
MUTABOR

Photography
Holger Wild

Design Office
MUTABOR HH

Principal Type
Bulldog and Buero 3000

Dimensions
15⁹⁄₁₆ x 8¹¹⁄₁₆ in. (39.5 x
22 cm)

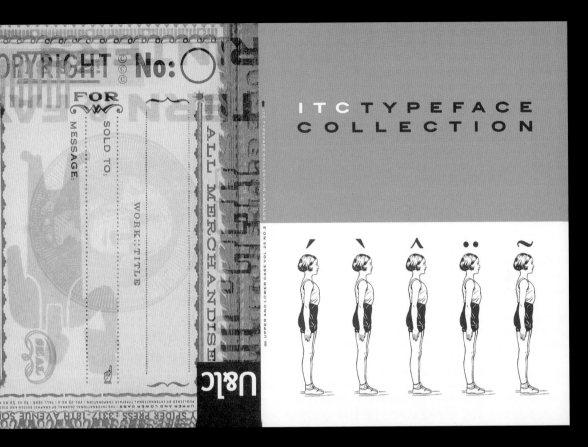

ITC TYPEFACE
COLLECTION

UPPER AND LOWER CASE : THE INTERNATIONAL JOURNAL OF GRAPHIC DESIGN AND DIGITAL
PUBLISHED BY INTERNATIONAL TYPEFACE CORPORATION : VOL.25 NO.2 : FALL 1998 : US $5 US $9.90

SPIDER PRESS : 331/ 18TH AVENUE SO

ITC TYPEFACE COLLECTION CATALOG

UPPER AND LOWER CASE VOL.25 NO.2

BEST AMERICAN GAY FICTION

2

EDITED BY BRIAN BOULDREY

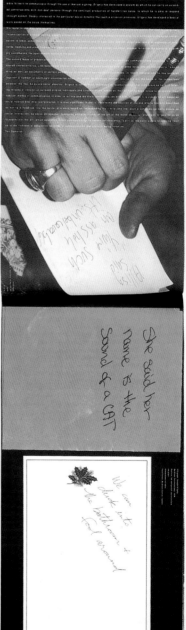

BOOK COVERS

. . . .

Design
Michael Ian Kaye and John
Fulbrook III
New York, New York

. . . .

Creative Direction
Michael Ian Kaye

. . . .

Photography
Daniel Bibb and Marc Tauss

. . . .

Studio
Little, Brown and Company

. . . .

Principal Type
Helvetica, Caslon, Univers,
ITC Quorum, and Odeon
Condensed

. . . .

Dimensions
Various

BOOK

. . . .

Design
Julia Hasting
London, England

. . . .

Art Direction
Alan Fletcher

. . . .

Studio
Phaidon Press

. . . .

Principal Type
DIN Mittelschrift

. . . .

Dimensions
7½ x 15 in. (19.1 x 38.1 cm)

CATALOG

. . . .

Design
Clifford Stoltze, Tammy
Dotson, Wing Ngan, and
Angelia Geyer
Boston, Massachusetts

Art Direction
Clifford Stoltze

. . . .

Studio
Stoltze Design

. . . .

Client
Massachusetts College of Art
and Design

. . . .

Principal Type
Futana Italic, Tasse,
Cornwall, and Mrs. Eaves

. . . .

Dimensions
8 x 11 in. (20.3 x 27.9 cm)

BROCHURE

. . . .

Design
Paul Ziller
San Francisco, California

. . . .

Art Direction
Paul Schulte

. . . .

Photo Illustration
Paul Ziller

. . . .

Studio
Schulte Design

. . . .

Client
San Francisco Ballet

. . . .

Principal Type
Zoinks, Comic, Spills, Active
Images, Bodega Sans, and
Franklin Gothic

. . . .

Dimensions
6³/₁₆ x 8¹/₄ in. (15.7 x 21 cm)

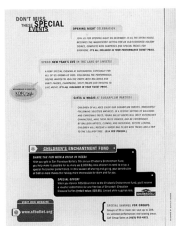

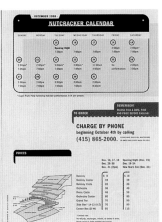

MISSION:
CITY PROJECTS IS A MULTIDISCIPLINARY
DIVISION OF THE CITY OF SYDNEY -
A TEAM CONSISTING OF URBAN DESIGNERS,
PROJECT MANAGERS, ARCHITECTS,
LANDSCAPE ARCHITECTS, PUBLIC ART
CURATORS AND INDUSTRIAL DESIGNERS.
A WIDE RANGE OF CONSULTANTS ARE ALSO
USED IN COLLABORATION. CITY PROJECTS
DRAWS IDEAS, CONCEPTS AND DESIGNS
FOR ITS PROJECTS FROM A LARGE NUMBER
OF PEOPLE, FROM SMALL YOUNG FIRMS
THROUGH TO LARGER ESTABLISHED
PRACTICES WITH DIVERSE BACKGROUNDS.
MANY OF THE PROJECTS INVOLVE ARTISTS
WORKING IN COLLABORATION OR DIRECTLY
ON THE DESIGN TEAM.

BROCHURE

Design
Zoë Wishart
Sydney, Australia

Art Direction
Zoë Wishart

Creative Direction
Zoë Wishart

Design Office
Wishart Design Pty. Ltd.

Client
City of Sydney/City Projects

Principal Type
Helvetica Condensed

Dimensions
$9^{11}/_{16}$ x $9^{11}/_{16}$ in. (24.5 x 24.5 cm)

BROCHURE

· · · · · · · · · · · · ·

Design
Kevin Roberson
San Francisco, California

· · · · · · · · · · · · ·

Art Direction
Bill Cahan

· · · · · · · · · · · · ·

Creative Direction
Bill Cahan

· · · · · · · · · · · · ·

Agency
Cahan & Associates

· · · · · · · · · · · · ·

Client
Bay Area World Trade
Center

· · · · · · · · · · · · ·

Principal Type
Gothic and Caslon

· · · · · · · · · · · · ·

Dimensions
9 x 12 in. (22.9 x 30.5 cm)

SHOPPING :
AN EXHIBITION
DEDICATED TO
THE ART OF BUYING.
IBM GALLERY NOV.

STUDENT WORK

· · · · · · · · · · · · ·

Design
Lisamarie Trombetta
Mastic, New York
· · · · · · · · · · · · ·

School
School of Visual Arts
· · · · · · · · · · · · ·

Instructor
Julian Peploe
· · · · · · · · · · · · ·

Principal Type
Dritz
· · · · · · · · · · · · ·

Dimensions
16 x 14 in. (40.6 x 35.6 cm)
· · · · · · · · · · · · ·

Third-place student winner

LAUNDRY BAG

· · · · · · · · · · · · ·

Design
Rafael Esquer
New York, New York
· · · · · · · · · · · · ·

Art Direction
Rafael Esquer
· · · · · · · · · · · · ·

Agency
@radical.media
· · · · · · · · · · · · ·

Principal Type
Interstate and Interstate
(modified)
· · · · · · · · · · · · ·

Dimensions
30 x 40 in. (76.2 x 101.6 cm)

this year
we thought it would be
better
to give than to receive

@radical.media

some of our
shirts, skirts, sweaters, pants & pullovers
have already been given to these organizations
and we hope
you'll do the same.

HEARTFELT FOUNDATION	**SAINT BENEDICT THE MOOR**
2101 Wilshire Boulevard Suite 103	283 Saint Anne's Avenue Ground Floor/Soup Kitchen
Santa Monica, CA 90403	**Bronx, NY 10454**
☏ **(310) 829.7857**	☏ **(718) 665.9693**

If you would like to participate, please call:

@radical.media	⇆	NY (212) 462-1500 Kathryn O'Kane
		LA (310) 664-4500 Denise Felloni

We'll coordinate all pick-ups... Happy New Year!

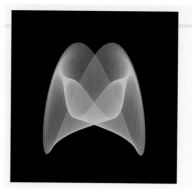

ANNUAL REPORT

· · · · · · · · · · · · ·

Design
Neal Ashby
Washington, D.C.

· · · · · · · · · · · · ·

Creative Direction
Neal Ashby

· · · · · · · · · · · · ·

Photography
Mike Northrup
Baltimore, Maryland

· · · · · · · · · · · · ·

Client
Recording Industry
Association of America

· · · · · · · · · · · · ·

Principal Type
Helvetica Neue and House
Gothic

· · · · · · · · · · · · ·

Dimensions
10 x 10 in. (25.4 x 25.4 cm)

BROCHURE

· · · · · · · · · · · · ·

Design
Gilmar Wendt
Bremen, Germany

· · · · · · · · · · · · ·

Art Direction
Gilmar Wendt

· · · · · · · · · · · · ·

Creative Direction
Rainer Groothuis and Victor
Malsy

· · · · · · · · · · · · ·

Agency
Groothuis & Malsy

· · · · · · · · · · · · ·

Principal Type
Foundry Wilson, Quadraat,
and Bell Gothic

· · · · · · · · · · · · ·

Dimensions
6 x 8¹¹/₁₆ in. (15.5 x 22 cm)

Design
Meiling Chen
New York, New York

School
School of Visual Arts

Instructor
Terry Koppel

Principal Type
Acropolis and Helvetica

Dimensions
17½ x 14¾ in. (44.5 x
37.5 cm)

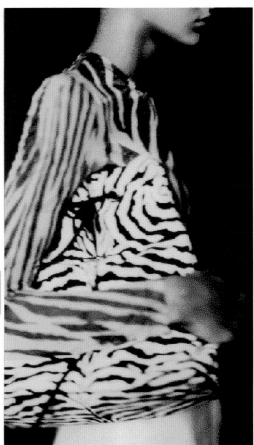

Lorem ipsum dolor sit amet, consectetuer adipiscing elit, sed diam nonummy nibh euismod tincidunt ut laoreet dolo magna

body
text
text
text

Lorem ipsum dolor sit amet, consectetuer adipiscing elit, sed diam nonummy nibh euismod tincidunt ut laoreet dolo magna aliquam erat volutpat. Ut wisi enim ad m

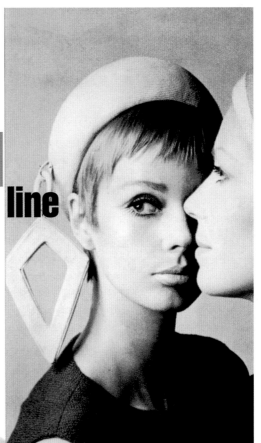

hard
line

PACKAGING
· · · · · · · · · · · · · · ·
Design
Johannes Plass
Hamburg, Germany
· · · · · · · · · · · · · · ·
Art Direction
Johannes Plass
· · · · · · · · · · · · · · ·
Illustration
Johannes Plass and Heinrich
Paravicini
· · · · · · · · · · · · · · ·
Studio
MUTABOR HH
· · · · · · · · · · · · · · ·
Client
Menzel Nolte Advertising
Agency
· · · · · · · · · · · · · · ·
Principal Type
Trade Gothic Extended and
Bureau Agency
· · · · · · · · · · · · · · ·
Dimensions
4^{11}/$_{16}$ x 2^9/$_{16}$ in. (11.8 x
6.5 cm)

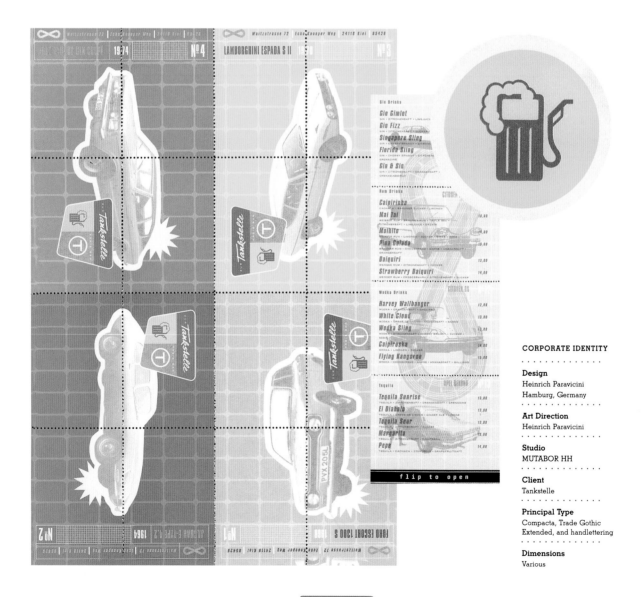

CORPORATE IDENTITY
· · · · · · · · · · · · · · ·
Design
Heinrich Paravicini
Hamburg, Germany
· · · · · · · · · · · · · · ·
Art Direction
Heinrich Paravicini
· · · · · · · · · · · · · · ·
Studio
MUTABOR HH
· · · · · · · · · · · · · · ·
Client
Tankstelle
· · · · · · · · · · · · · · ·
Principal Type
Compacta, Trade Gothic
Extended, and handlettering
· · · · · · · · · · · · · · ·
Dimensions
Various

MAGAZINE
. . . .
Design
Mike Joyce and Kelly Hogg
New York, New York
. . . .
Art Direction
Katherine Phelps
. . . .
Creative Direction
Vicky Pedlak
. . . .
Studio
Platinum Design, Inc.
. . . .
Client
BOMB
. . . .
Principal Type
Bell Gothic and FF Scala
. . . .
Dimensions
8⅝ x 10⅝ in. (22.6 x
27.6 cm)

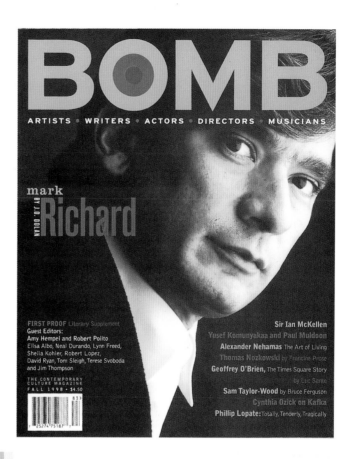

Thomas Nozkowski

BY FRANCINE PROSE

One of the reasons I was so eager to interview Tom Nozkowski (who's been a friend and whose work I've admired for twenty years) is that I imagined that I might finally begin to understand what makes his paintings—inventive, often brightly colored abstractions on small panels—so beautiful, mysterious, surprising and unique, so simultaneously and paradoxically whimsical and haunting. But of course, our illuminating conversation—like any true education—only deepened, or intensified, the mystery. Our talk, which took place at the kitchen table overlooking the garden of Tom's house in the Hudson Valley, got started after we'd cleared away the stacks and stacks of books (on literature, art, travel and gardening) that he'd bought the previous day at our local library fair.

Francine Prose is the author of nine novels, two story collections and most recently, a collection of novellas, *Guided Tours of Hell*.

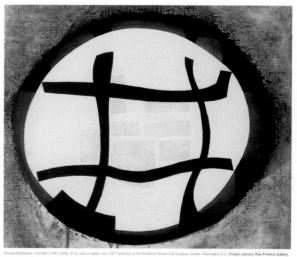

Thomas Nozkowski, *Untitled (7-84)*, 1996, Oil on linen on panel, 16 × 20″. Collection of the Hirshhorn Museum & Sculpture Garden, Washington D.C.. Images courtesy Max Protetch Gallery.

CATALOG

. . . .

Design
David Bull, Oscar
Fernández, M. Christopher
Jones, and Andreas Kranz
Columbus, Ohio

. . . .

Design Direction
Oscar Fernández

. . . .

Agency
VIA, Inc.

. . . .

Client
Columbus Society of
Communicating Arts

. . . .

Principal Type
ITC Officina Sans and ITC
Officina Serif

. . . .

Dimensions
8½ x 8 in. (21.6 x 20.3 cm)

▶

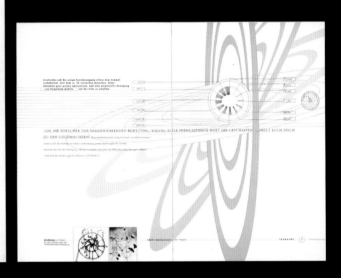

STUDENT WORK

. . . .

Design
Anja Wesner
Stuttgart, Germany

. . . .

School
Staatliche Akademie der
Bildenden Künste Stuttgart

. . . .

Principal Type
Stempel Schneidler, Triplex
Sans, and Triplex Serif

. . . .

Dimensions
8⅝ x 13 in. (22 x 33 cm)

. . . .

First-place student winner

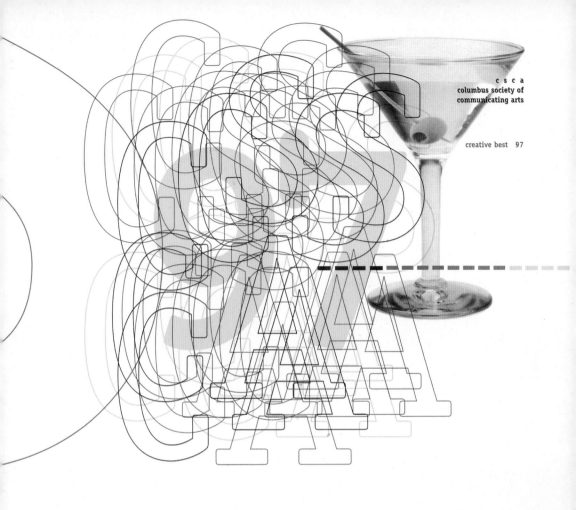

c s c a
**columbus society of
communicating arts**

creative best 97

---

writing   The Shortest Book You'll
         Ever Read About
         Networking Technology

designer   Crit Warren
writer   George Felton
photographer   Crit Warren, Stock Photography
printer   West-Camp Press, Inc.
organization   Schmeltz+Warren
client   Babbage-Simmel,
audience   MIS Employees & Business
                  Managers

Gone are the mainframe empires of uniformity. It's unity now, not uniformity, and its strength lies in diversity.

Computers aren't inside with the I.S. people anymore; they're out here with everybody else.

We're all teachers now. Information is diffuse. So is power. (The king is dead. Long live the kings.)

But too many people look out at their computer users and think,"If a little knowledge is a dangerous thing, just how much trouble am I in?

We look out there and think just how good a start that knowledge is. Let's make more.

Maybe the glass is neither half full nor half empty. It just needs more ice.

LOGOTYPE

Design
Deborah Hom
San Diego, California

Art Direction
John Ball

Creative Direction
John Ball

Design Office
Mires Design, Inc.

Client
Nike, Inc.

Principal Type
Agency

ZINE SPREAD

n
oodward and Gail
on
ork, New York

ection
oodward

graphy
Seliger

Editor
Knepfer

Stone

al Type
ia

sions
in. (30.5 x 50.8 cm)

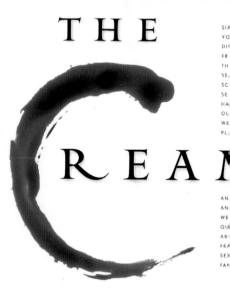

THE

S REAM

TEAM

BY ERIK HEDEGAARD

CAMPAIGN

Design
Mark Denton
London, England

Creative Direction
Mark Denton

Typographer
Andy Dymock

Design Office
Typeworks

Client
Bonce

Principal Type
Bell Copperplate

Dimensions
5⁵/₁₆ x 7¾ in. (13.5 x 19.7 cm)

INVITATION

Design
Troy Tyner
Winston-Salem,
North Carolina

Art Direction
Troy Tyner

Writer
Stephen Young

Agency
Henderson Tyner Art Co.

Client
Studio Place Photography

Principal Type
Lubalin Graph, Compacta,
Eurostile, Housebroken, and
OptiScript

Dimensions
7 x 7 in. (17.8 x 17.8 cm)

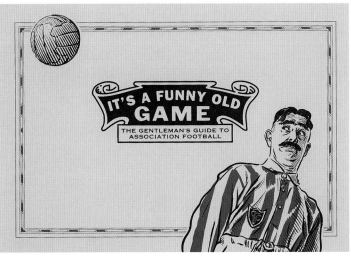

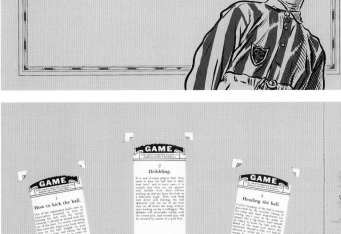

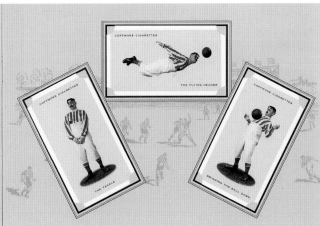

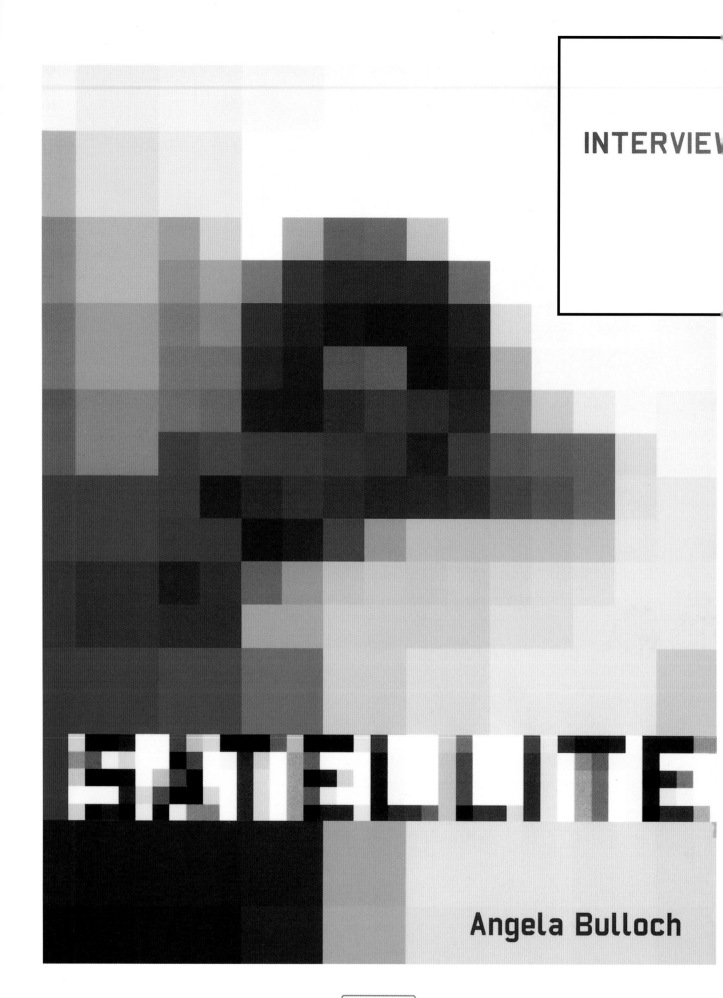

INTERVIEW

SATELLITE

Angela Bulloch

BOOK

. . . .

Design
Christian Küsters
London, England

. . . .

Studio
CHK Design Ltd.

. . . .

Client
Museum of Contemporary
Arts, Zurich

. . . .

Principal Type
AF Carplates and
AF Satellite

. . . .

Dimensions
7½ x 9½ in. (19 x 24 cm)

ANNUAL REPORT

. . . .

Design
Heike Lichte
Berlin, Germany

. . . .

Lettering
Petra Beisse

. . . .

Art Direction
Klaus Fehsenfeld

. . . .

Creative Direction
Klaus Fehsenfeld

. . . .

Photography
Wolfgang Scholvien and
Thomas Peschel

. . . .

Agency
W. A. F. Werbegesellschaft
GmbH

. . . .

Client
Deutsche Handelsbank AG

. . . .

Principal Type
Slimbach and Frutiger

. . . .

Dimensions
8¼ x 11⅝ in. (21 x 29.7 cm)

Vintage: Typography

BROCHURE
. . . .

Design
Kit Hinrichs and Brian
Jacobs
San Francisco, California

Creative Direction
Kit Hinrichs

Studio
Pentagram Design, Inc.

Client
Potlatch Corporation

Principal Type
News Gothic
. . . .

Dimensions
6¾ x 9¾ in. (17.2 x 24.8 cm)

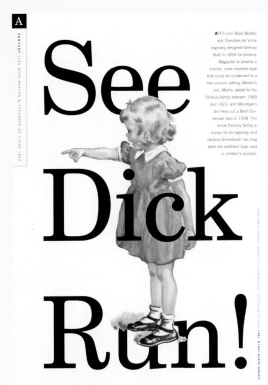

ATF's Linn Boyd Benton and Theodore de Vinne originally designed Century Bold in 1894 for *Century Magazine* to provide a blacker, more readable type that could be condensed to a two-column setting. Benton's son, Morris, added to the Century family between 1900 and 1923, and Monotype's Sol Hess cut a Bold Condensed face in 1938. The entire Century family is known for its legibility, and Century Schoolbook has long been the preferred type used in children's primers.

18

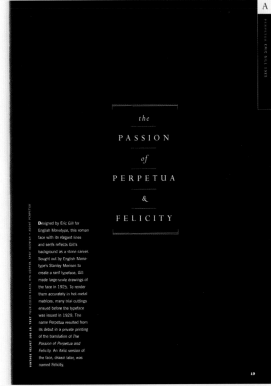

the
PASSION
of
PERPETUA
&
FELICITY

Designed by Eric Gill for English Monotype, this roman face with its elegant lines and serifs reflects Gill's background as a stone carver. Sought out by English Monotype's Stanley Morison to create a serif typeface, Gill made large-scale drawings of the face in 1925. To render them accurately in hot-metal matrices, many trial cuttings ensued before the typeface was issued in 1929. The name Perpetua resulted from its debut in a private printing of the translation of *The Passion of Perpetua and Felicity*. An italic version of the face, drawn later, was named Felicity.

19

the Teens

JEEPERS

It's Jake With Me

Whizzbang

Heaven to Betsy!

OVER THE TOP

BlackJack!

TypeSpec

Design
Giorgio Pesce
Lausanne, Switzerland

Lettering
Giorgio Pesce

Art Direction
Giorgio Pesce

Creative Direction
Giorgio Pesce

Agency
Atelier Poisson

Client
Rouge de Honte

Principal Type
Eurostile

Dimensions
Various

INVITATION

Design
Mike Jasinski and John Avila
Chicago, Illinois

Art Direction
John Avila

Creative Direction
John Avila and Mary Ackerly

Agency
Edelman Worldwide

Client
Motorola Corporation

Principal Type
Syntax and Democratica

Dimensions
5¼ x 8 in. (13.3 x 20.3 cm)

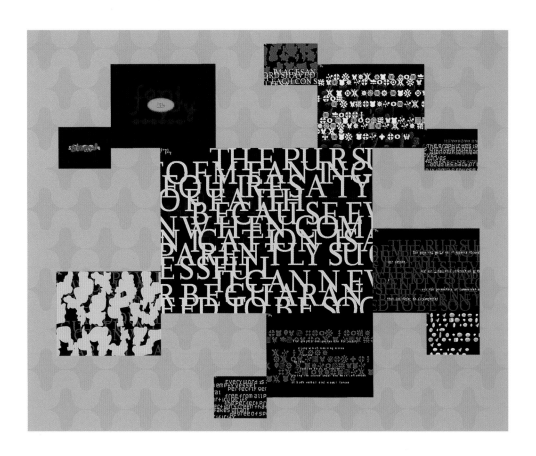

SCREEN SAVER

• • • • • • • • • • • • •

Design
Bob Aufuldish
San Anselmo, California
• • • • • • • • • • • • •

Programmers
David Karam and Dave
Granvold
San Francisco, California
• • • • • • • • • • • • •

Writer
Mark Bartlett
Oakland, California
• • • • • • • • • • • • •

Sound Designer
Bob Aufuldish
• • • • • • • • • • • • •

Design Office
Aufuldish & Warinner
• • • • • • • • • • • • •

Client
fontBoy.com
• • • • • • • • • • • • •

Principal Type
Armature, Avalanche, Baufy,
Panspermia, Punctual,
RoarShock, Viscosity, and
Whiplash

VIDEO
. . . .

Lettering
Oliver Bock
Hamburg, Germany
. . . .

Creative Direction
Arndt Dallmann and Guido
Heffels
. . . .

Director
Oliver Bock
. . . .

Producer
Jörg Bittel and Jassna Sroka
. . . .

Agency
Springer & Jacoby Werbung
GmbH
. . . .

Client
Markenfilm Filmproduction
. . . .

Principal Type
Times Roman

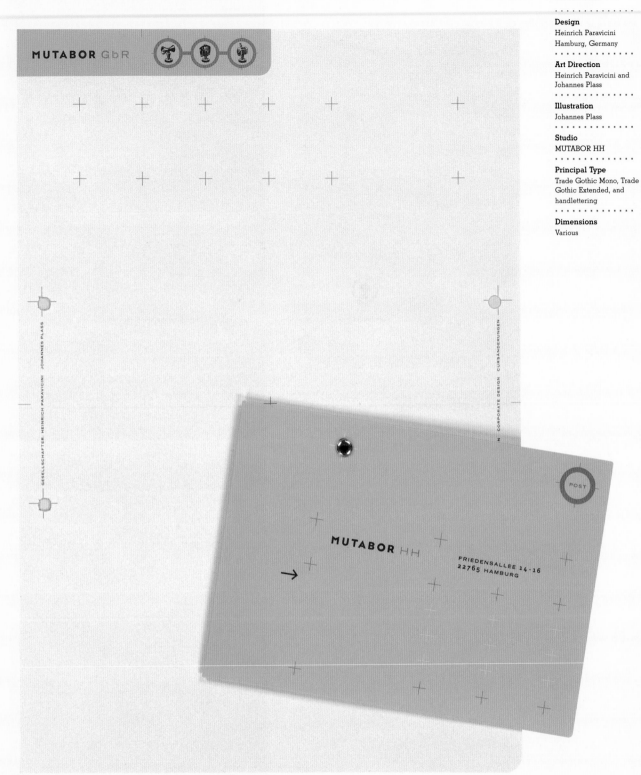

Design
Heinrich Paravicini
Hamburg, Germany

Art Direction
Heinrich Paravicini and
Johannes Plass

Illustration
Johannes Plass

Studio
MUTABOR HH

Principal Type
Trade Gothic Mono, Trade
Gothic Extended, and
handlettering

Dimensions
Various

STATIONERY

Design
Carlos Segura
Chicago, Illinois

Art Direction
Carlos Segura

Creative Direction
Carlos Segura

Letterpress
Rohner Letterpress

Design Office
Segura, Inc.

Client
Glow

Principal Type
FF Isonorm and custom type

Dimensions
8½ x 11 in. (21.6 x 27.9 cm)

A CREATIVE COMMUNICATIONS AGENCY.

GLOW. A CREATIVE COMMUNICATIONS AGENCY. 400 SOUTH EL CAMINO REAL. SUITE 400. SAN MATEO. CALIFORNIA 94402. USA.

400 SOUTH EL CAMINO REAL. SUITE 400. SAN MATEO. CALIFORNIA 94402. USA. 650.548.6950 (t) 650.548.6955 (f) WWW.GLOWSF.COM

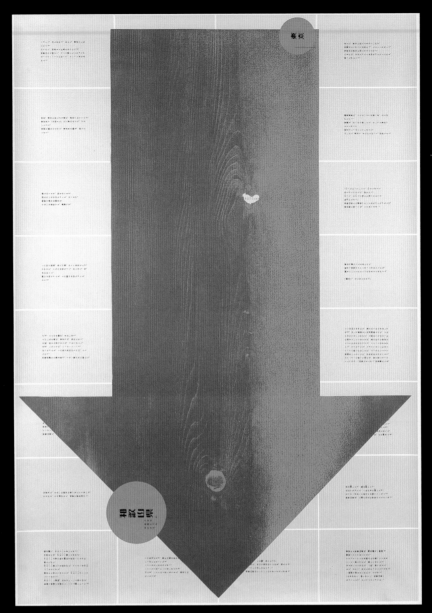

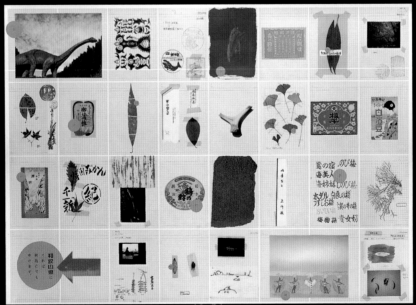

POSTER

Design
Hiroaki Nagai
Tokyo, Japan

· Art Direction
Hiroaki Nagai

Creative Direction
Daisaku Fujiwara

Photography
Tamotsu Fujii

Copywriter
Daisaku Fujiwara

Design Office
N.G., Inc.

Client
Wakayama Prefecture

Principal Type
Various

Dimensions
57 1/8 x 40 9/16 in. (145.6 x
103 cm)

POSTER
. . . .
Design
Cho Hyun
Seoul, Korea
. . . .
Art Direction
Cho Hyun
. . . .
Studio
Mad Braun
. . . .
Client
Yoon Design Institute
. . . .
Principal Type
CB Univers 67 Condensed
Bold
. . . .
Dimensions
28¾ x 39⅜ in. (73 x 100 cm)

BOOK
. . . .
Design
Gilmar Wendt
Bremen, Germany
. . . .
Art Direction
Victor Malsy and Gilmar
Wendt
. . . .
Agency
Groothuis + Malsy
. . . .
Client
Dumont Buchverlag
. . . .
Principal Type
News Gothic
. . . .
Dimensions
5⁹⁄₁₆ x 8⁵⁄₁₆ in. (14.2 x
21.2 cm)

. . . .

Design
Pacey Chao
Taipei, Taiwan

. . . .

Creative Direction
Van So

. . . .

Photography
Lo Tung-Chiang

. . . .

Production
China Blue

. . . .

Agency
JRV International Company

. . . .

Client
Yageo Corporation

. . . .

Principal Type
OCR-B and Copperplate

. . . .

Dimensions
3¾ x 3¾ in. (9.5 x 9.5 cm)

STATIONERY

. . . .

Design
Darina Geiling
Baltimore, Maryland

. . . .

Art Direction
Anthony Rutka

. . . .

Design Studio
Rutka Weadock Design

. . . .

Principal Type
Alternate Gothic, Interstate,
Century Schoolbook,
Blackoak, and Orator

. . . .

Dimensions
8½ x 11 in. (21.6 x 27.9 cm)

◄

CAMPAIGN

. . . .

Design
Florian Schoffro and Olaf
Stein
Hamburg, Germany

. . . .

Art Direction
Uwe Melichar and Olaf Stein

. . . .

Design Office
Factor Design

. . . .

Principal Type
Alternate Gothic and
Sackers Gothic

. . . .

Dimensions
Various

The McDonaldization of Business

ETHiCS

The world struggles toward a global definition of right and wrong.
By Laurie Joan Aron

MAGAZINE SPREAD
. . . .

Design
Tom Brown and Sarah Vinas
Coquitlam, British Columbia,
Canada and New York,
New York
. . . .

Art Direction
Tom Brown
. . . .

Studio
Deloitte & Touche
. . . .

Principal Type
Interstate and Electra
. . . .

Dimensions
12 x 17 in. (30.5 x 43.2 cm)

Design
Paul Sahre
Brooklyn, New Yo

Art Direction
Knickerbocker

Copywriter
Jesse Gordon

Design Office
Office of Paul Sah

Client
Nozone

Principal Type
Trade Gothic

Dimensions
24 x 36 in. (61 x 9

"My favorite season of work is Spring, only because I find people are generally more content ... and because I'm a Therapist and a Bartender, that makes me happy." —Therapist/Bartender

IN THIS ISSUE — DEHUMANIZATION. EXPLOITATION. DESPAIR. COFFEE. *Featuring:* Steven Ahlgren, Ron Barrett, Gary Baseman, Benoît, Blex Bolex, Gary Clement, Lloyd Dangle, Jesse Gordon, Knickerbocker, Lobrow, Mark Marek, Christoph Niemann, Particle 17, David Plunkert, Brian Rea, P. Revess, Johnathon Rosen, Paul Sahre, Scott Stowell, Ed Subitzky, Johnny Sweetwater, Takeshi Tadatsu.

NOZONE #8 WORK

Nozone Magazine P.O. Box 1124, Knickerbocker Station, New York NY 10002 USA

Design
Ben Pham
San Francisco, California

Art Direction
Bill Cahan

Creative Direction
Bill Cahan

Agency
Cahan & Associates

Client
Zeum

Principal Type
Trade Gothic and Adobe
Garamond

Dimensions
2½ x 2½ x 5 in. (6.4 x 6.4 x
12.7 cm)

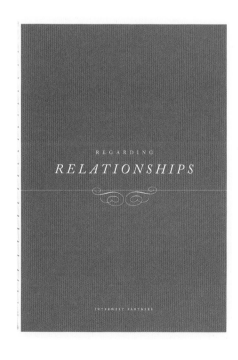

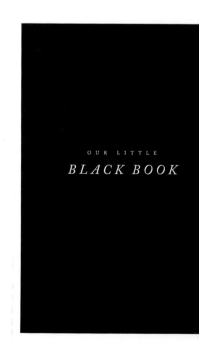

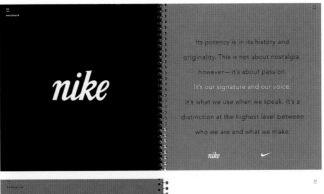

BROCHURE

Design
Valerie Taylor-Smith
Beaverton, Oregon

Art Direction
Valerie Taylor-Smith

Creative Direction
Valerie Taylor-Smith

Writer
Denny Wendt

Production
Trish Fitzpatrick

Printing
Irwin Hodsen
Portland, Oregon

Client
Nike, Inc.

Principal Type
Avenir

Dimensions
6⅜ x 6⅛ in. (16.2 x 15.6 cm)

ON PROSPERITY

BE
HUMBLE
IN THE
FACE OF
SUCCESS.

*Building a highly successful company is the
ultimate achievement for you as an entrepreneur.
We'll do everything we can to help, but we do so with
the conviction that the credit belongs to you.*

FLIP GIANOS

BROCHURE

Design
Kevin Roberson
San Francisco, California

Art Direction
Bill Cahan

Creative Direction
Bill Cahan

Agency
Cahan & Associates

Client
Interwest Partners

Principal Type
Caslon and Clarendon

Dimensions
6¾ x 9½ in. (17.2 x 24.1 cm)

Folha de S. Paulo Newspaper. Illustrating life with words for 77 years.

Folha de S.Paulo Newspaper. Illustrating life with words for 77 years.

ナゾの即席ラーメン展

湯気のむこうに宇宙がみえる

協力＝日清食品㈱／㈱新横浜ラーメン博物館

監修＝町田忍

入場無料

開館時間＝11:00〜19:00

主催＝TOTO食の情報館RECIPE

7月2日[木]─9月1日[火]

TOTO食の情報館RECIPE 5F食のギャラリー

休館日＝8月5日[木]・13日[木]〜16日[日]

TOTO RECIPE

TOTO食の情報館RECIPE 〒104-0061東京都中央区銀座7-8-7 Tel.03-3573-1009 インターネットのホームページでもご案内しています。http://www.toto.co.jp/RECIPE/

· · · · · · · · · · · · ·

Design
Keiko Hirano
Chuo-ku, Tokyo, Japan
· · · · · · · · · · · · ·

Art Direction
Keiko Hirano
· · · · · · · · · · · · ·

Photography
Takashi Homma
· · · · · · · · · · · · ·

Design Office
Hirano Studio, Inc.
· · · · · · · · · · · · ·

Client
Victor Entertainment, Inc.
· · · · · · · · · · · · ·

Principal Type
Univers and ChuGothicBBB1
· · · · · · · · · · · · ·

Dimensions
5 x 5⁹⁄₁₆ in. (12.6 x 14.2 cm)

POSTER
· · · · · · · · · · · · ·

Design
Masayoshi Kodaira
Tokyo, Japan
· · · · · · · · · · · · ·

Art Direction
Masayoshi Kodaira
· · · · · · · · · · · · ·

Design Office
Masayoshi Kodaira Design
Office
· · · · · · · · · · · · ·

Client
TOTO Co., Ltd.
· · · · · · · · · · · · ·

Principal Type
Oblong, CBSK1, and
handlettering
· · · · · · · · · · · · ·

Dimensions
40½ x 28⅝ in. (103 x
72.8 cm)

CAMPAIGN

. . . .

Design
Jason Schulte
Minneapolis, Minnesota

. . . .

Art Direction
Charles S. Anderson

. . . .

Copywriter
Jason Schulte

. . . .

Studio
Charles S. Anderson Design
Company

. . . .

Client
French Paper Company

. . . .

Principal Type
Arena Black Extended and
Trade Gothic

. . . .

Dimensions
Various

COMEDY CENTRAL'S *traditional Canadian*

MIDNIGHT BREAKFAST

FRIDAY·JULY 24TH 1998
11:59 PM·THE DELTA HOTEL

MIDNIGHT

HASH BROWNS

BACON

EGGS

"BREAKFAST AT MIDNIGHT? THIS MUST BE SOME KIND OF TYPO."
This, no doubt, will be the question on a tourist's mind while visiting Canada.

CANADA IS NOT AMERICA, AND THEREFORE IT IS DIFFERENT. THIS IS A FACT THAT SHOULD NOT JUST BE PUSHED ASIDE. AND SO WITH THAT IN MIND, NOT ONLY IS COMEDY CENTRAL HOSTING A TRADITIONAL CANADIAN MIDNIGHT BREAKFAST, (SEE ABOVE) IT IS ALSO PROVIDING GUESTS WITH THIS HANDY POCKET GUIDE (SEE BELOW) TO SOME OF THE OTHER MANY MYSTERIES THAT MAKE CANADA THE WONDER THAT IT IS. ENJOY AND BENEFIT FROM OUR KNOWLEDGE.

CARTOGRAPHERS BELIEVE CANADA TO BE SOMEWHERE ON THE TOP HALF OF THIS PLANET.

POPULATION: Who's counting, and frankly, who cares?

FAVORITE FOOD: Hummus

FAVORITE COLOR: Blue

LIKES: fancy cars, nice dinners, moonlight walks on the beach, and quality time with the dog.

DISLIKES: racists, mean people. (They suck.)

THE UNITED STATES

DO NOT BE AFRAID.
Canadians can smell fear. Hold out your hand, palm forward, and let them reach out and shake your hand. This will tell them that you are "friendly."

Canadians communicate through a series of clicks and pops made by moving their tongues and jaws. It can be difficult to understand, but it has a musical quality that is quite lovely. HERE ARE SOME COMMON ENGLISH PHRASES AND THEIR CANADIAN EQUIVALENTS. YOU MIGHT FIND THIS HELPFUL.

AMERICAN ENGLISH	CANADIAN TRANSLATION
Greetings.	Howdee!
Me llamo Paco.	Me llamo Paco.
Please don't touch me there.	Eh, no thank you?
In my country this would be illegal.	Kiss my grits!
I enjoy Comedy Central.	Can you get me free South Park stuff?

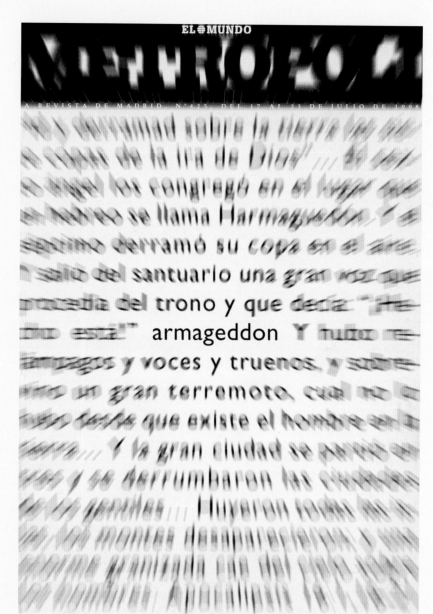

MAGAZINE

Design
Rodrigo Sánchez
Madrid, Spain

Art Direction
Rodrigo Sánchez

Creative Direction
Carmelo Caderot

Studio
Unidad Editorial, S.A.

Client
El Mundo

Principal Type
Giza Seven Nine, Gill Sans,
and Cloister

Dimensions
7⅞ x 11¼ in. (20 x 28.5 cm)

POSTER

Design
Paula Scher, Anke
Stohlmann, and Keith Daigle
New York, New York

Lettering
Paula Scher

Art Direction
Paula Scher

Studio
Pentagram Design

Client
The Public Theater

Principal Type
Handlettering

Dimensions
48 x 36 in. (121.9 x 91.4 cm)

▶

JOYOUS!
JACK TINKER
LONDON DAILY MAIL
MAGIC!
MICHAEL SOMMERS
THE STAR LEDGER
ELEGANT!
JOHN LAHR, THE NEW YORKER
ELECTRIC!
BEN BRANTLEY
THE NEW YORK TIMES
GENIUS!
JOEL SIEGEL
WABC TV
GLORIOUS!
LAURA SHAPIRO
NEWSWEEK
BRING IN 'DA
NOISE
BRING IN 'DA
FUNK
LINDA WINER
NEWSDAY
BREAKTHROUGH!
WONDERFUL!!
CLIVE BARNES, N.Y. POST
HEAR 'DA FUNK ON RCA VICTOR
EXPLOSIVE!
HOWARD KISSEL
DAILY NEWS
MICHAEL KUCHWARA
ASSOCIATED PRESS
SIZZLING!!
THE PUBLIC THEATER ON BROADWAY
P
WINNER OF 4 1996 TONY AWARDS
CALL TELE-CHARGE IN NY NJ CT 212-239-6200 OUTSIDE N.Y. METRO AREA 800-432-7250
25 THE AMBASSADOR THEATRE 219 WEST 49 TH ST.

Leon de Winter

op de weg

CALENDAR

. . . .

Design
Bau Winkel
The Hague, The Netherlands

. . . .

Art Direction
Bau Winkel

. . . .

Creative Direction
Bau Winkel

. . . .

Studio
Studio Bau Winkel

. . . .

Client
Ando

. . . .

Principal Type
Bembo

. . . .

Dimensions
7⅝ x 9¹¹⁄₁₆ in. (20 x 24.5 cm)

BOOK

· · · · · · · · · · · · · · ·

Design
Julia Sedykh
Boston, Massachusetts

· · · · · · · · · · · · · · ·

Lettering
Julia Sedykh

· · · · · · · · · · · · · · ·

Art Direction
Michael Ian Kaye
New York, New York

· · · · · · · · · · · · · · ·

Creative Direction
Michael Ian Kaye

· · · · · · · · · · · · · · ·

Publisher
Little, Brown and Company

· · · · · · · · · · · · · · ·

Principal Type
Historical Allsorts Fell Types,
TheSans, and Whirligig

· · · · · · · · · · · · · · ·

Dimensions
4⅝ x 7⁵⁄₁₆ in. (12.8 x
18.6 cm)

TO WIN A BET

Light seven green candles and say:

Abracadabra
Abracadabr
Abracadab
Abracada
Abraca
Abrac
Abr
Ab
A

[76]

Repeat seven times and extinguish the candle. Do this for seven days. When you place your bet you are more likely to win.

THE LOTTERY

The Romanies often like to gamble, and they advise using this spell for the lottery.

Light one green candle for each of the numbers to be selected. Sit quietly and ponder the flames, allowing each flame in turn to suggest a number.

Fill in the form according to the numbers that come into your head. Sprinkle the sheet with nutmeg and then snuff out the candles. Leave the form dusted with nutmeg for a day before thoroughly brushing it off.

[77]

Tradition says
that if you drop money and
someone else picks it up for you
and puts it in your hands,
it is an omen of more money to come.

It is unlucky for the recipient
of a gift of a purse or wallet
not to receive a coin inside it.

RETAIL ENVIRONMENT GUIDE

AMERICAN HERITAGE

LEGACY–PRIDE–HISTORY–HONOR
AUTHENTICITY–H·D FOREVER

*Muted colors, classic typography, and
archival images tell the intertwining tales of Harley-Davidson
and American motorcycling.*

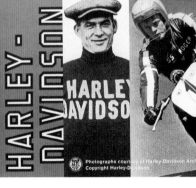

BOOK
· · · · · · · · · · · · · ·
Design
Rob Hicks
Chicago, Illinois

Creative Direction
Curt Schreiber
· · · · · · · · · · · · · ·
Consultant
Michael Davidson
New York, New York
· · · · · · · · · · · · · ·
Design Office
VSA Partners
· · · · · · · · · · · · · ·
Client
Harley-Davidson Motor Co.
· · · · · · · · · · · · · ·
Principal Type
Bulmer and Akzidenz
Grotesk
· · · · · · · · · · · · · ·
Dimensions
5½ x 8½ in. (14 x 21.6 cm)

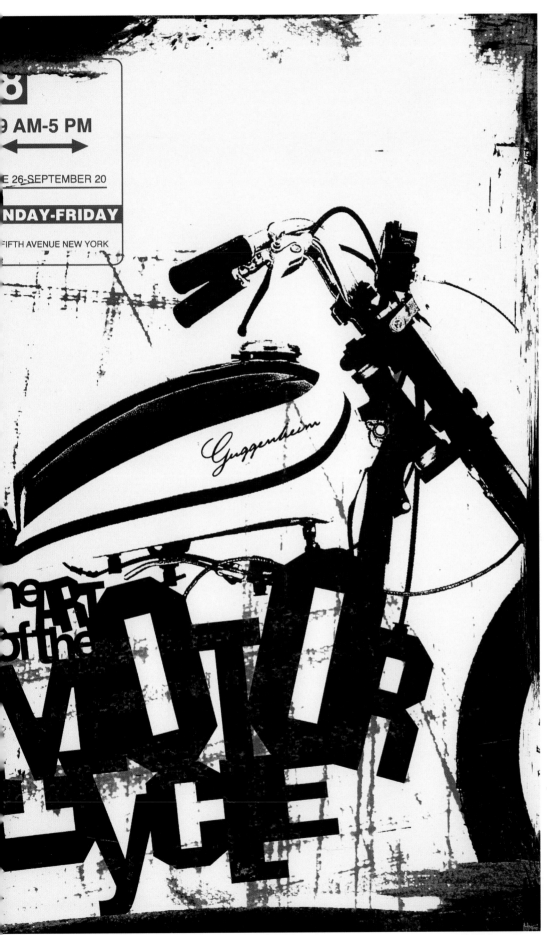

8

9 AM-5 PM

←→

E 26-SEPTEMBER 20

NDAY-FRIDAY

FIFTH AVENUE NEW YORK

Guggenheim

he ART
of the
MOTOR
CYCLE

STUDENT WORK
. . . .
Design
Tien-Chieh Chang
New York, New York
. . . .
School
School of Visual Arts
. . . .
Instructor
Carin Goldberg
. . . .
Principal Type
ITC Machine and Helvetica
. . . .
Dimensions
11 x 16½ in. (27.9 x 41.9 cm)

STATIONERY

Design
Sharon Werner
Minneapolis, Minnesota

Art Direction
Sharon Werner

Studio
Werner Design Werks, Inc.

Client
Joanie Bernstein, Art Rep

Principal Type
Clarendon and Univers
Extended

Dimensions
6½ x 10¼ in. (16.5 x 26 cm)

ANNUAL REPORT

Design
Marion English
Birmingham, Alabama

Lettering
Marion English

Art Direction
Marion English

Creative Direction
Marion English

Photography
Don Harbor

Agency
Slaughter Hanson

Client
Central Alabama Council of
the Boy Scouts of America

Principal Type
Venetian

Dimensions
8¼ x 8½ in. (21 x 21.6 cm)

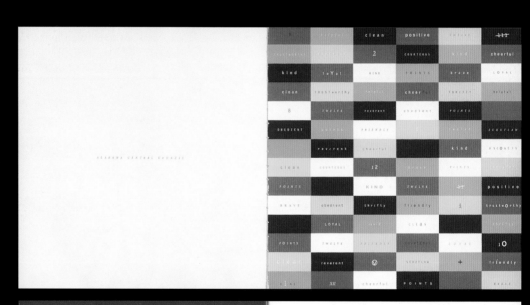

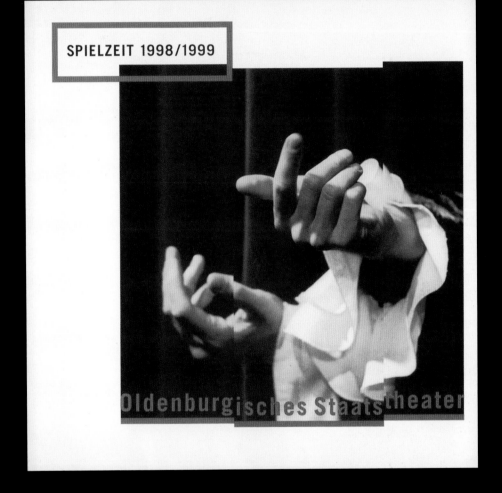

CATALOG

Design
Ulrike Kleine-Ebeling and
Fons M. Hickmann
Düsseldorf, Germany

Art Direction
Fons M. Hickmann and
Ulrike Kleine-Ebeling

Editor
Anke Hoffmann

Client
Oldenburgisches
Staatstheater

Principal Type
Trade Gothic and Joanna

Dimensions
9 x 9 in. (23 x 23 cm)

Photographs by HUGH HALES-TOOKE
Fashion by DERICK PROCOPE

ALTERED EGOS

Traditional suits say you're professional and in control no matter how surreal your life seems. Time-honored suits in crisp pinstripes or solids are a stress-free approach to office dressing, whether you're climbing the corporate ladder on Wall Street or the walls at home

Wool-blend suit by Giorgio Armani, $2,080. Cotton shirt by Emporio Armani, $195. Tie by Tommy Hilfiger Collection. Shoes by Donna Karan.

OCTOBER 1998 • DETAILS 183

MAGAZINE SPREAD

Design
Alden Wallace
New York, New York

Design Direction
Robert Newman

Client
Details

Principal Type
Akzidenz Grotesk and Clarendon

Dimensions
8 x 10 in. (20.3 x 25.4 cm)

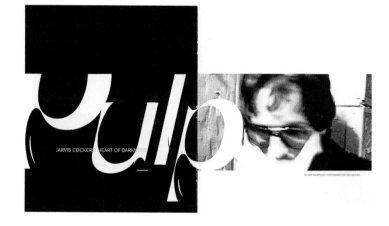

JARVIS COCKER'S HEART OF DARKNESS

MAGAZINE SPREAD

Design
David Yamada
New York, New York

Art Direction
David Yamada

Photography
Ken Schles

Client
Request Media

Principal Type
Pulp

Dimensions
20 x 11⅜ in. (50.8 x 28.9 cm)

BOOK

. . . .

Design

Phil Baines, Darren Hughes,
Barry Hurd, David Jury, Alan
Kitching, Robert Park-
Barnard, Kelvyn Smith, and
Jeremy Tankard
London, England

Art Direction

David Jury
Manningtree, Essex, England

Photography

Humphrey Spender
Near Hatfield Peveral, Essex,
England

. . . .

Studio

Colchester Institute and
Foxash Studios

. . . .

Client

Foxash Publishing

. . . .

Principal Type

Gill Sans

. . . .

Dimensions

20⅝ x 15 in. (53 x 38 cm)

BOOKPLATES

. . . .

Design
Rachael Dinnis
Twickenham, England
. . . .

Art Direction
Domenic Lippa and Harry
Pearce
. . . .

Creative Direction
Domenic Lippa and Harry
Pearce
. . . .

Photography
Paul Reeves
. . . .

Design Studio
Lippa Pearce Design Ltd.
. . . .

Client
Lippa Pearce Design Ltd.
. . . .

Principal Type
Crillie
. . . .

Dimensions
4½ x 6 in. (11.4 x 15.2 cm)

Bookplate ('buk.pleit) *A label, usually pasted inside the front cover of a book, bearing the name or crest of the ...ating ownership.*

24 - bookplates, 8 - different designs, 3 - of each
25p from each pack will be donated to the Lawyers Committee for
Human Rights. Designed and produced by Lippa Pearce Design,
358a Richmond Road, Twickenham, TW1 2DU. T 0181 744 2100.

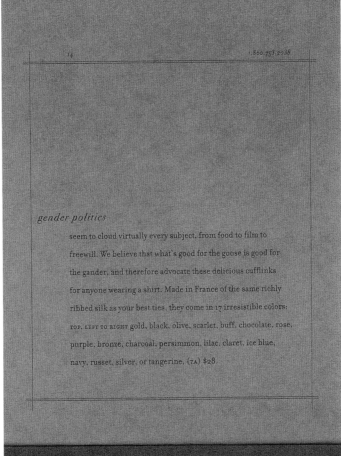

gender politics

seem to cloud virtually every subject, from food to film to
freewill. We believe that what's good for the goose is good for
the gander, and therefore advocate these delicious cufflinks
for anyone wearing a shirt. Made in France of the same richly
ribbed silk as your best ties, they come in 17 irresistible colors:
TOP, LEFT TO RIGHT gold, black, olive, scarlet, buff, chocolate, rose,
purple, bronze, charcoal, persimmon, lilac, claret, ice blue,
navy, russet, silver, or tangerine. (7A) $28.

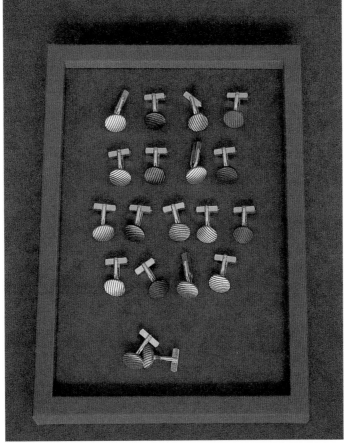

CATALOG

. . . .

Design
Allison Muench Williams
New York, New York

. . . .

Creative Direction
Allison Muench Williams
and J. Phillips Williams

. . . .

Photography
Maria Robledo

. . . .

Design Office
design:m/w

. . . .

Client
Takashimaya New York

. . . .

Principal Type
Filosofia

. . . .

Dimensions
5⅝ x 9 in. (14.3 x 22.9 cm)

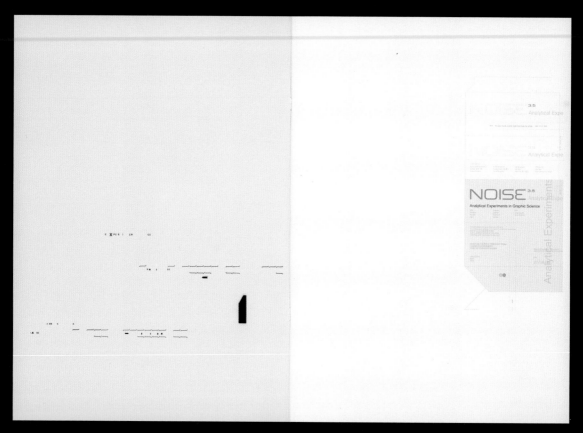

BOOK

Design
The Attik
Huddersfield and London,
England, New York,
New York, San Francisco,
California, and Sydney,
Australia

Art Direction
Aporva Baxi
London, England

Creative Direction
Simon Needham and James
Sommerville
Sydney, Australia and
New York, New York

Studio
The Attik

Principal Type
Enabler Thin, Univers, and
Stem/2c Stencil

Dimensions
16½ x 11¾ in. (41.9 x
29.9 cm)

MAGAZINE

. . . .

Design
Garth Walker, Siobhan
Gunning, Brode Vosloo,
William Rea, Russell Stark,
Lisa King, Deanne Wynne,
Anelia Schutte, Barry
Downard, Jean Hofmeyer,
Sheila Dorje, Wilhelm
Kruger, Peter Hudson,
Brandt Botes, Rikus Ferreira,
Carl Addy, and Mark
Tomlinson
Durban, South Africa

. . . .

Creative Direction
Garth Walker

. . . .

Agency
Orange Juice Design

. . . .

Client
Ogilvy & Mather

. . . .

Principal Type
Various

. . . .

Dimensions
11 11/16 x 16 1/2 in. (29.7 x
42 cm)

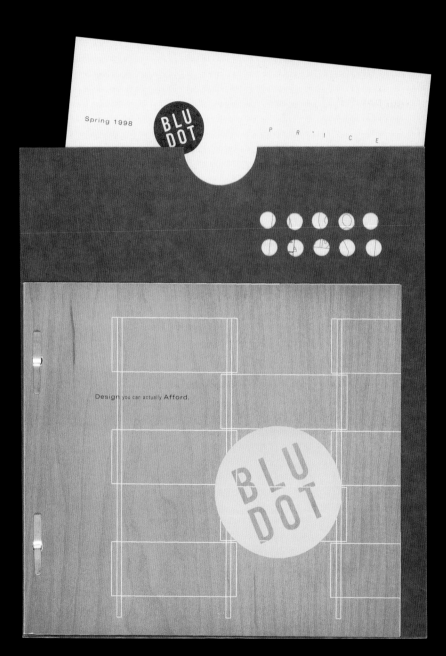

CATALOG

Design
Sharon Werner and Sarah Nelson
Minneapolis, Minnesota

Art Direction
Sharon Werner

Studio
Werner Design Werks, Inc.

Client
Blu Dot Design and Manufacturing

Principal Type
News Gothic and Univers Extended

Dimensions
9⅝ x 11¼ in. (24.5 x 28.6 cm)

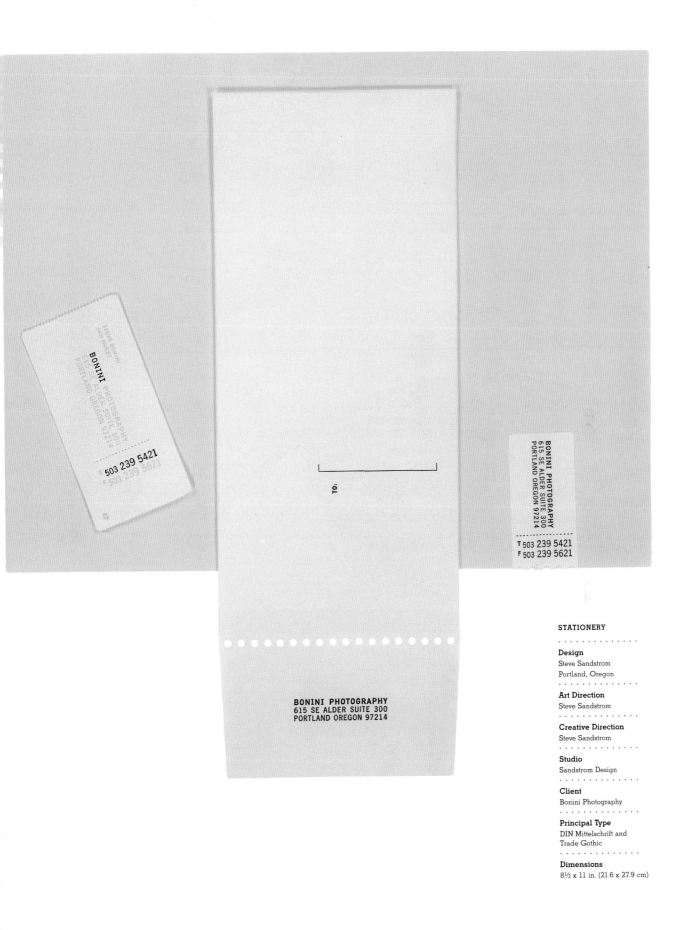

TO:

BONINI PHOTOGRAPHY
615 SE ALDER SUITE 300
PORTLAND OREGON 97214

STEVE BONINI
JAN BINSEY

BONINI PHOTOGRAPHY
615 SE ALDER SUITE 300
PORTLAND OREGON 97214

T 503 239 5421
F 503 239 5621

BONINI PHOTOGRAPHY
615 SE ALDER SUITE 300
PORTLAND OREGON 97214

T 503 239 5421
F 503 239 5621

STATIONERY
. . . .

Design
Steve Sandstrom
Portland, Oregon
. . . .

Art Direction
Steve Sandstrom
. . . .

Creative Direction
Steve Sandstrom
. . . .

Studio
Sandstrom Design
. . . .

Client
Bonini Photography
. . . .

Principal Type
DIN Mittelschrift and
Trade Gothic
. . . .

Dimensions
8½ x 11 in. (21.6 x 27.9 cm)

Letter from the Editor

Coffee Black

ADVERTISING

NOTES OF INTERVIEW WITH TROY AND JIM

the beginning

the marriage

the clients

the future

from one write to another

what they want you to know

the issues

end of tape.

WordSong Been Here. WordSay Gone.

duane michals

Joseph Cornell

BY: VICKI YOUNG

WHATZNU

Rough's "WhatzNu" covers industry news, people, and events. So, WhatzNu with you? Pictures are OK too.
Mail: Vicki Young • 1400 Turtle Creek Blvd. #206 • Dallas, Texas 75207 • Fax: 214.741.6563 • email: youngco@flash.net

NEW MEMBERS

Want to join DSVC?
call Sue Reynolds at 972-241-2017
or fax to 972-247-8735

Roughage

ORBITING THE GIANT HAIRBALL

PHIL'S CALENDAR

SO MILLION WOMEN MARCH

PHIL'S MILLENNIUM RECOMMENDATIONS

INSPIRATION CAN'T HAPPEN IF YOU RUN OUT OF RESOURCES.

YaHOO
GRAPHIC ART SUPPLIES

BROCHURE

. . . .

Design
Alejandro Melguiro, Ariel
Eroles, and Ezequiel
Abramson
Buenos Aires, Argentina

. . . .

Art Direction
Carolina Bilbao and
Santiago Felipelli

. . . .

Creative Direction
Monica Halpert

. . . .

Agency
Bridger/Conway

. . . .

Design Office
Cisneros Television Group

. . . .

Principal Type
Letter Gothic, DIN
Engschrift, Democratica,
Loco Type, and Ariston Bold

. . . .

Dimensions
14¼ x 9½ in. (36.2 x
24.1 cm)

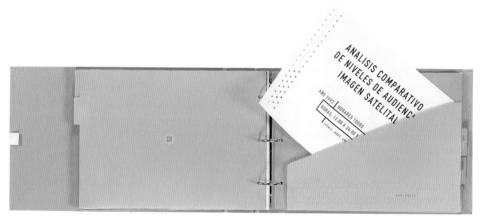

MAGAZINE

. . . .

Design
Scott Ray, Chad Hoffheins,
Jan Wilson, Pham Nhan, and
Dorit Suffness
Dallas, Texas

. . . .

Art Direction
Pham Nhan

. . . .

Creative Direction
Pham Nhan

. . . .

Agency
Peterson & Company

. . . .

Client
Dallas Society of Visual
Communications

. . . .

Principal Type
Bell Gothic

. . . .

Dimensions
23⅝ x 36 in. (60 x 91.4 cm)

PACKAGING

. . . .

Design
Haley Johnson
Minneapolis, Minnesota
. . . .

Lettering
Haley Johnson
. . . .

Copywriters
Mitch Nash, Gerry D'Amour,
and Lisa McConnell
. . . .

Studio
Haley Johnson Design
Company
. . . .

Client
Blue Q
. . . .

Principal Type
Handlettering
. . . .

Dimensions
4 x 2½ x 1½ in. (10.2 x 6.4 x
3.8 cm)

▼

PACKAGING

. . . .

Design
Haley Johnson
Minneapolis, Minnesota
. . . .

Copywriters
Gerry D'Amour, Haley
Johnson, and Richard
Casucci
. . . .

Studio
Haley Johnson Design
Company
. . . .

Client
Blue Q
. . . .

Principal Type
Trade Gothic (modified)
. . . .

Dimensions
4 x 2½ x 1½ in. (10.2 x 6.4 x
3.8 cm)

LOGOTYPE

. . . .

Design
Vittorio Costarella
Seattle, Washington
. . . .

Lettering
Vittorio Costarella
. . . .

Art Direction
Vittorio Costarella
. . . .

Studio
Modern Dog
. . . .

Principal Type
Helvetica Neue and
handlettering

STUDENT WORK

· · · · · · · · · · · · · · ·

Design
Daisuke Endo
New York, New York

· · · · · · · · · · · · · · ·

School
School of Visual Arts

· · · · · · · · · · · · · · ·

Instructor
Carin Goldberg

· · · · · · · · · · · · · · ·

Principal Type
Univers Condensed

· · · · · · · · · · · · · · ·

Dimensions
4 x 4 x 4½ in. (10.2 x 10.2 x
11.4 cm)

· · · · · · · · · · · · · · ·

Second-place student winner

BUTTERFLY FRENCH

BIG ED FRENCH

FAULD FRENCH

FANGS FRENCH

RAINSONG FRENCH

KING NILES FRENCH

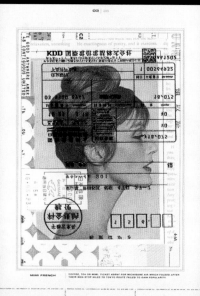

MIMI FRENCH

EARL FRENCH

YEK FRENCH

Client
Rhythm & Hues

Principal Type
Rockwell, Interstate, Franklin
Gothic, News Gothic, Zapf
Dingbats, and Mrs. Eaves

Dimensions
Various

PROMOTION

Design
Charles S. Anderson, Todd

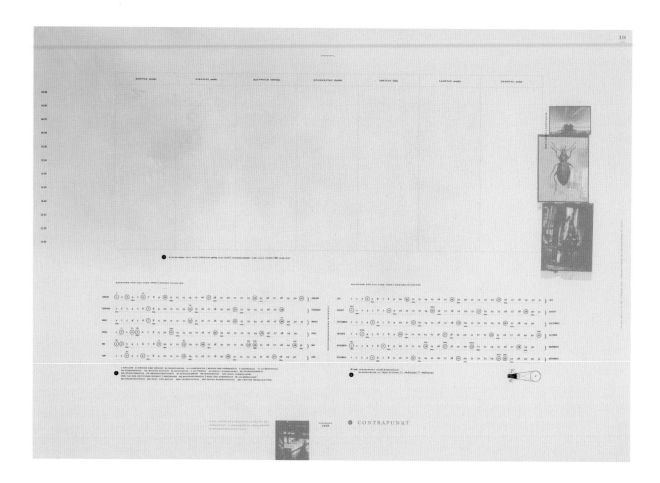

CALENDAR

. . . .

Design
Patrick Vallee
Munich, Germany

. . . .

Art Direction
Patrick Vallee and Emmo
Reiss

. . . .

Photography
Patrick Vallee and Emmo
Reiss

. . . .

Studio
Patrick Vallee Design

. . . .

Client
Contrapunkt

. . . .

Principal Type
Adobe Garamond, Trade
Gothic, Democratica, and
Engravers LH

. . . .

Dimensions
23¼ x 16⅝ in. (59 x 42 cm)

DIARY
· · · · · · · · · · · · · · · · · ·

Design
Petra Černe Oven
Ljubljana, Slovenia

Lettering
Lucijan Bratuš
· · · · · · · · · · · · · · · · · ·

Art Direction
Petra Černe Oven
· · · · · · · · · · · · · · · · · ·

Creative Direction
Petra Černe Oven
· · · · · · · · · · · · · · · · · ·

Editor
Jerneja Batič
· · · · · · · · · · · · · · · · · ·

Studio
Studio Id
· · · · · · · · · · · · · · · · · ·

Client
Ministry of Culture of the
Republic of Slovenia,
Cultural Heritage Office
· · · · · · · · · · · · · · · · · ·

Principal Type
Columbus
· · · · · · · · · · · · · · · · · ·

Dimensions
5 13/16 x 8¾ in. (14.8 x
22.2 cm)

SCORPIO

23. 10. - 22. 11. 1999 / 23. 10. - 22. 11. 2000 / 23. 10. - 22. 11. 2001

NOVEMBER

November / Listopad November je po rimskem koledarju deveti
mesec. Latinsko *novem* pomeni devet. Kot veliko drugih mesecev v
letu je tudi november pri nas dobil ime glede na dogajanje v naravi.
Imenujemo ga LISTOPAD saj se v tem času rastlinje poslavlja, kar
ponazarja odpadanje listja.

November According to the Roman calendar
October is the ninth month of the year.
Novem denotes nine in Latin. Like many
other months, Slovenes named it after what
occurs in nature during this period. This is
the month in which vegetation withers and
leaves fall from trees, and is therefore called
LISTOPAD (from list=leaf, padati=to fall) in
Slovene.

ANNUAL REPORT

. . . .

Design
Kevin Roberson
San Francisco, California

. . . .

Art Direction
Bill Cahan

. . . .

Creative Direction
Bill Cahan

. . . .

Agency
Cahan & Associates

. . . .

Client
Heartport

. . . .

Principal Type
Trade Gothic and Trade
Gothic Bold Condensed

. . . .

Dimensions
5 x 7 in. (12.7 x 17.8 cm)

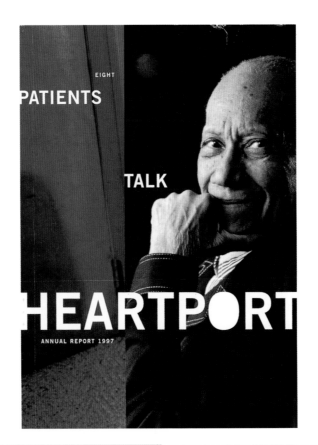

EIGHT

PATIENTS

TALK

HEARTPORT

ANNUAL REPORT 1997

SECTIONS 1-2-11-1
TO SECTIONS 3-4-14-1

SHELBYVILLE HIGH

I DREADED HAVING
HEART SURGERY,
ESPECIALLY BECAUSE I HAD
NO SYMPTOMS. I EXERCISE
A LOT, AND AM VERY
ACTIVE, YET I NEVER
NOTICED ANY PAIN. BUT
TESTS SHOWED I NEEDED
FOUR VESSELS BYPASSED.

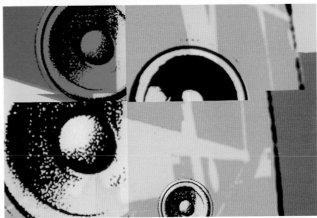

TV OPENING

Design
Bucky Fukumoto
Santa Monica, California

Lettering
Bucky Fukumoto

Art Direction
Vanessa Marzaroli

Creative Direction
Seth Epstein

Animation
Craig Tollifson

Producer
Jen Earle

Executive Producer
Moody Glasgow

Studio
Fuel

Client
MTV Networks

Principal Type
Handlettering

Homage to Paul Rand   Message from Kan Tai-keung 靳埭強 Hong Kong, China

CAMPAIGN
. . . .
Design
Alexander Gelman
New York, New York
. . . .
Art Direction
Alexander Gelman
. . . .
Studio
Design Machine
. . . .
Client
Obscure Objects, Five Fifty
Five, and Design Machine
. . . .
Principal Type
Century
. . . .
Dimensions
31½ x 22½ in. (80 x
57.2 cm)

POSTER
. . . .
Design
Kan Tai-keung
Hong Kong, China
. . . .
Lettering
Kan Tai-keung
. . . .
Art Direction
Kan Tai-keung
. . . .
Creative Direction
Kan Tai-keung
. . . .
Computer Illustration
Benson Kwun Tin Yau
. . . .
Agency
Kan & Lau Design
Consultants
. . . .
Principal Type
Futura Regular, Mono Mtlei
Medium, and handlettering
. . . .
Dimensions
23⁷/₁₆ x 16⁹/₁₆ in. (59.5 x
42 cm)

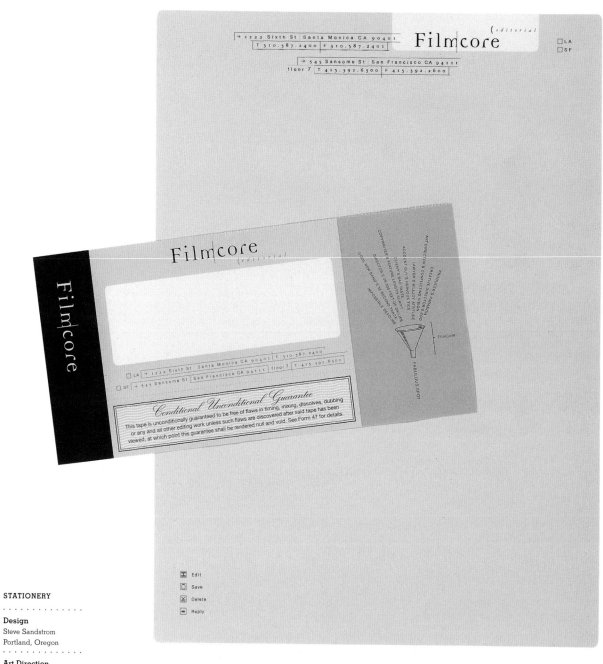

166 T D C 20

STATIONERY

. . . .

Design
Steve Sandstrom
Portland, Oregon
. . . .

Art Direction
Steve Sandstrom
. . . .

Creative Direction
Steve Sandstrom
. . . .

Studio
Sandstrom Design
. . . .

Client
Filmcore
. . . .

Principal Type
Democratica, Garamond
No. 3, and Helvetica Neue
. . . .

Dimensions
8½ x 11 in. (21.6 x 27.9 cm)

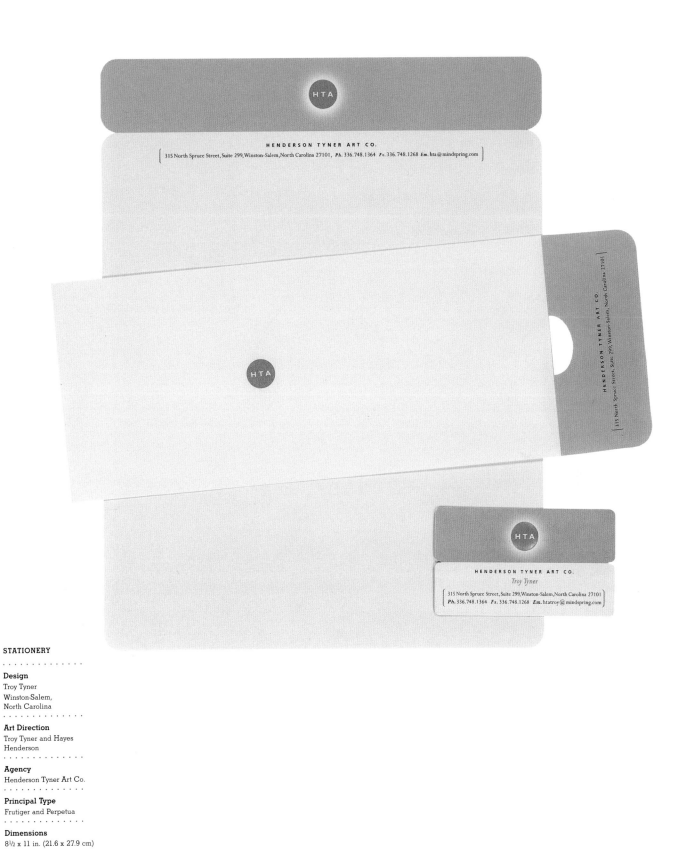

STATIONERY

- - - - - - - - - - - -

Design
Troy Tyner
Winston-Salem,
North Carolina
- - - - - - - - - - - -

Art Direction
Troy Tyner and Hayes
Henderson
- - - - - - - - - - - -

Agency
Henderson Tyner Art Co.
- - - - - - - - - - - -

Principal Type
Frutiger and Perpetua
- - - - - - - - - - - -

Dimensions
8½ x 11 in. (21.6 x 27.9 cm)

STUDENT WORK

Design
Lorena Llaneza
New York, New York

School
School of Visual Arts

Instructor
Chris Austopchuk

Principal Type
Helvetica Neue, Univers, and
Stencil

Dimensions
Various

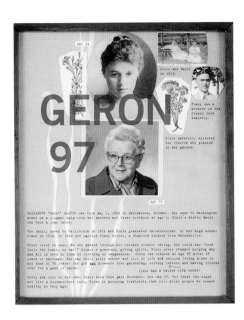

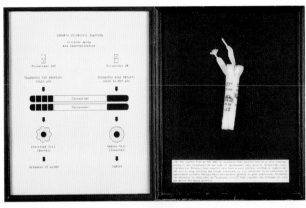

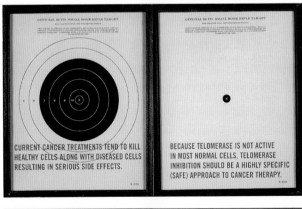

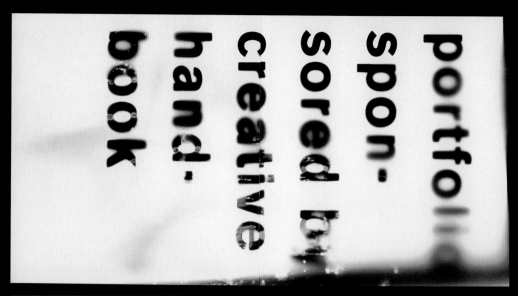

BOOK

. . . .

Design
Jacques Koeweiden and Ralf
Schroeder
Amsterdam, The Netherlands
. . . .

Art Direction
Jacques Koeweiden
. . . .

Creative Direction
Jacques Koeweiden
. . . .

Design Office
Koeweiden Postma
Associates
. . . .

Client
Photography Association of
the Netherlands
. . . .

Principal Type
Akzidenz Grotesk
. . . .

Dimensions
12 x 11¼ in. (30.5 x 28.5 cm)

TV OPENING

Design
Julian Grey
Toronto, Ontario, Canada

Art Direction
Julian Grey

Creative Direction
Julian Grey

Studio
Head Gear Animation, In

Client
Sundance Channel

Principal Type
Schableon (modified)

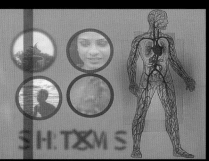

DOMINGO 3PM A
DE ETIQUETA NEGRA
Lunes Especial
MGD
TODOS LOS JUEGOS
2 por $1.00
¡NO NECESITA CUPONES!
DE ETIQUETA NEGRA
Lunes Especial
PAGUE $4.95 POR PERSONA
Y RECIBA
Miller
JUEGOS ILIMITADOS
3PM A 9PM
DE ETIQUETA NEGRA
MODERACION

POSTER

. . . .

Design
Hal Wolverton and Heath
Lowe
Portland, Oregon

. . . .

Lettering
Hal Wolverton, Heath Lowe,
Joe Peila, Sarah Starr, Alan
Foster, Neil Gust, Mary
Kysar, and Topher Sinkinson

. . . .

Art Direction
Hal Wolverton and Heath
Lowe

. . . .

Creative Direction
Alicia Johnson and Hal
Wolverton

. . . .

Photography
Melody McDaniel
Los Angeles, California

. . . .

Agency
Wieden & Kennedy

. . . .

Studio
Johnson & Wolverton

. . . .

Client
Miller Brewing Co.

. . . .

Principal Type
Champion (modified)

. . . .

Dimensions
20 x 30 in. (50.8 x 76.2 cm)

CORPORATE IDENTITY

. . . .

Design
Michael Hodgson
Santa Monica, California

. . . .

Art Direction
Michael Hodgson and Clive
Piercy

. . . .

Creative Direction
Michael Hodgson and Clive
Piercy

. . . .

Artist
Huntley Muir
Cirencester, England

. . . .

Design Office
Ph.D

. . . .

Client
Ciudad

. . . .

Principal Type
Eurostile Bold Condensed,
Matrix Script Book, Latin,
Rockwell Bold Condensed,
Tarzana, and handlettering

. . . .

Dimensions
Various

CD-ROM

. . . .

Design
Olivier Chetelat
San Francisco, California

. . . .

Creative Direction
Terry Irwin and Rick Lowe

. . . .

Production Specialist
Regina Serrambana

. . . .

Agency
MetaDesign

. . . .

Principal Type
Crank Call

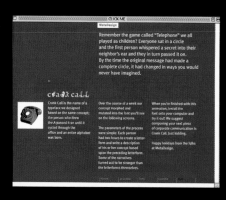

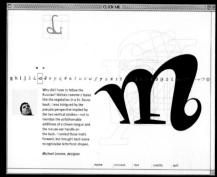

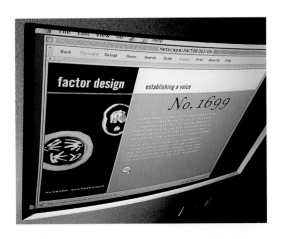

WEB SITE
. . . .

Design
Andrea Herstowski and Jeff
Zwerner
San Francisco, California
. . . .

Art Direction
Jeff Zwerner
. . . .

Studio
Factor Design, San Francisco
. . . .

Client
Factor Design, Hamburg and
San Francisco
. . . .

Principal Type
Alternate Gothic and
Sackers Heavy Gothic

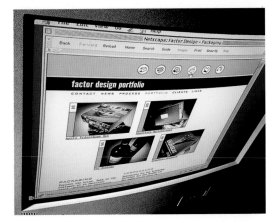

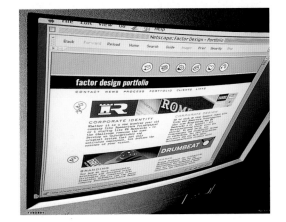

POSTER

· · · · · · · · · · · · ·

Design
Patrick Giasson
Montréal, Québec, Canada

· · · · · · · · · · · · ·

Art Direction
Patrick Giasson

· · · · · · · · · · · · ·

Photography
Diana Shearwood

· · · · · · · · · · · · ·

Agency
Behaviour Design

· · · · · · · · · · · · ·

Client
TGR Zone

· · · · · · · · · · · · ·

Principal Type
Core

· · · · · · · · · · · · ·

Dimensions
59 x 42 in. (149.9 x
106.7 cm)

BROCHURE

· · · · · · · · · · · · · ·

Design
Lea Nichols and David
Cannon
Atlanta, Georgia

· · · · · · · · · · · · · ·

Creative Direction
Phil Hamlett

· · · · · · · · · · · · · ·

Photography
Greg Slater

· · · · · · · · · · · · · ·

Copywriter
Robert Roth

· · · · · · · · · · · · · ·

Design Office
EAI/Atlanta

· · · · · · · · · · · · · ·

Client
Dickson's/Williamson

· · · · · · · · · · · · · ·

Principal Type
Helvetica Neue Condensed
and Clarendon

· · · · · · · · · · · · · ·

Dimensions
6 x 8 in. (15.2 x 20.3 cm)

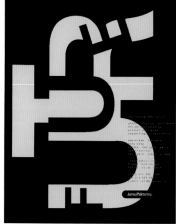

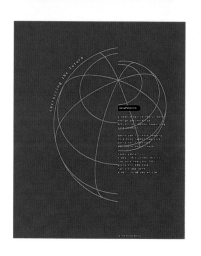

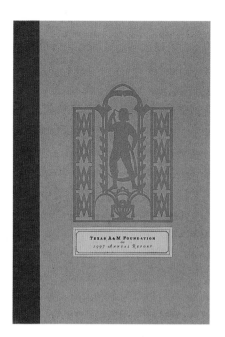

ANNUAL REPORT

. . . .

Design
Mark Geer and Jeffrey
W. Savage
Houston, Texas

. . . .

Art Direction
Mark Geer

. . . .

Design Studio
Geer Design, Inc.

. . . .

Client
Texas A&M Foundation

. . . .

Principal Type
Clarendon, Caslon, and
Caslon Italic

. . . .

Dimensions
7 x 10¼ in. (17.8 x 26 cm)

CAMPAIGN

. . . .

Design
Alexander Gelman
New York, New York

. . . .

Creative Direction
Alexander Gelman

. . . .

Studio
Design Machine

. . . .

Client
Janou Pakter, Inc.

. . . .

Principal Type
DIN Mittelschrift Alt,
Akzidenz Grotesk, and
Univers

. . . .

Dimensions
Various

◄

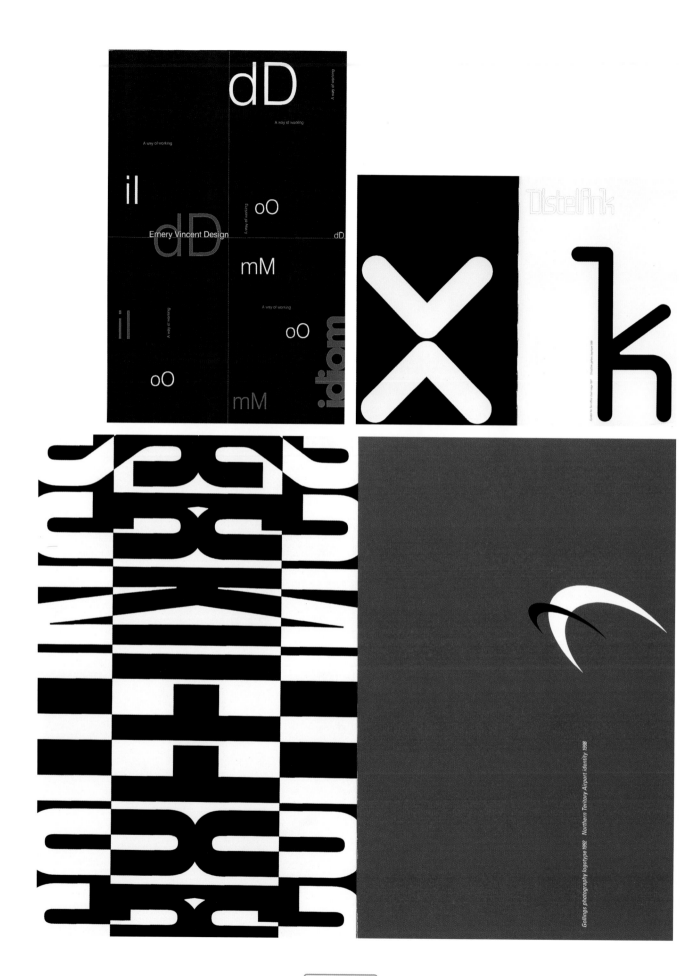

ANNUAL REPORT
. . . .

Design
Valerie Taylor-Smith
Beaverton, Oregon
. . . .

Art Direction
Valerie Taylor-Smith
. . . .

Creative Direction
Valerie Taylor-Smith and Bob
Lambie
. . . .

Editorial
Bob Lambie and Stanley
Hainsworth
. . . .

Printing
Acme Printing
Boston, Massachusetts
. . . .

Production
Ann Riedl
. . . .

Client
Nike, Inc.
. . . .

Principal Type
Avenir
. . . .

Dimensions
8½ x 11 in. (21.6 x 27.9 cm)

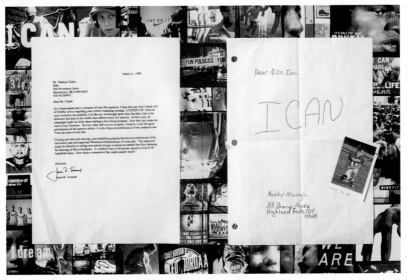

BROCHURE
. . . .

Design
Emery Vincent Design
Melbourne, Victoria,
Australia
. . . .

Art Direction
Garry Emery
. . . .

Creative Direction
Garry Emery
. . . .

Studio
Emery Vincent Design
. . . .

Principal Type
Univers and Futura
. . . .

Dimensions
6⅛ x 9¼ in. (15.7 x 23.5 cm)

◄

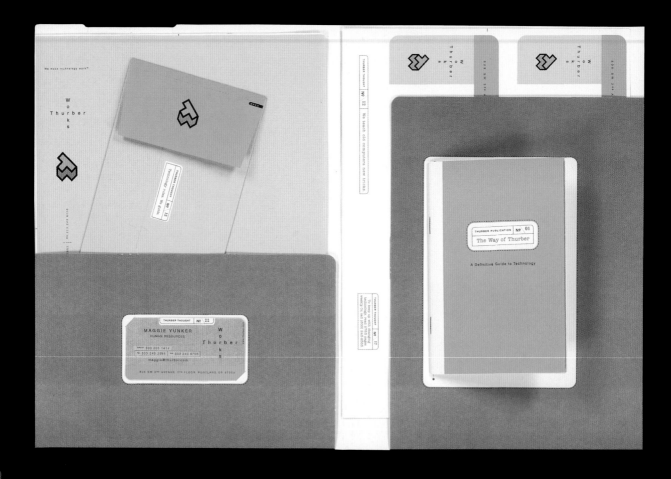

STATIONERY

. . . .

Design
Jon Olsen
Portland, Oregon

. . . .

Art Direction
Jon Olsen

. . . .

Creative Direction
Steve Sandstrom

. . . .

Copywriter
Leslie Dillon

. . . .

Studio
Sandstrom Design

. . . .

Client
Thurberworks

. . . .

Principal Type
Helvetica and Garamond
No. 3

. . . .

Dimensions
8½ x 11 in. (21.6 x 27.9 cm)

BOOK

Design
Sebastian Bissinger and
Nikolai Wolff
Bremen, Germany

Art Direction
Professor Eckhard Jung

Creative Direction
Professor Eckhard Jung

Studio
Hochschule für Künste
Bremen

Client
Arbeitsgemeinschaft für
Friedens und
Konfliktforschung

Principal Type
Berthold Bodoni and Quay
Sans

Dimensions
10 x 12¼ in. (25.5 x 31 cm)

THE ★ PULSE

PLANS ON FUTURE:
DTWN**2010**

Downtown Minneapolis in the year 2010. A place whose diverse economic and social cultures have continued to evolve upon the solid foundations we forge today. Where corporations, humanities, educational interests, marketplaces and individuals converge into one culture. An active, open haven in the heart of it all. Where the economy and the population thrive together in harmony.

Follow along through this glimpse of Downtown Minneapolis 2010. Imagine you're there. See how this cultural evolution will work to make us

DOWN TOWN

M O R E

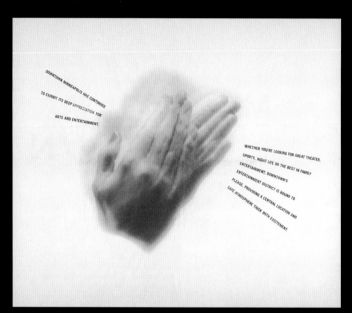

DOWNTOWN MINNEAPOLIS HAS CONTINUED
TO EXHIBIT ITS DEEP APPRECIATION FOR
ARTS AND ENTERTAINMENT.

WHETHER YOU'RE LOOKING FOR GREAT THEATER, SPORTS, NIGHT LIFE OR THE BEST IN FAMILY ENTERTAINMENT, DOWNTOWN'S ENTERTAINMENT DISTRICT IS BOUND TO PLEASE, PROVIDING A CENTRAL LOCATION AND SAFE ATMOSPHERE THICK WITH EXCITEMENT.

BROCHURE

. . . .
Design
David Schrimpf
Minneapolis, Minnesota
. . . .
Creative Direction
Bill Thorburn
. . . .
Photography
Chuck Smith Photography
. . . .
Copywriter
Michael Cronin
. . . .
Agency
Carmichael Lynch Thorburn
. . . .
Client
Downtown Council of
Minneapolis
. . . .
Principal Type
Baskerville and Concho
. . . .
Dimensions
13½ x 11½ in. (34.3 x
29.2 cm)

THE EXPANDED CORPORATE CULTURE FEEDS SURROUNDING RETAILERS A STEADY DIET OF HUNGRY CUSTOMERS.

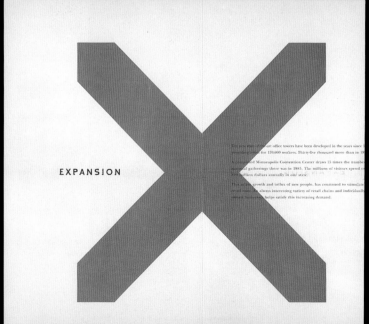

EXPANSION

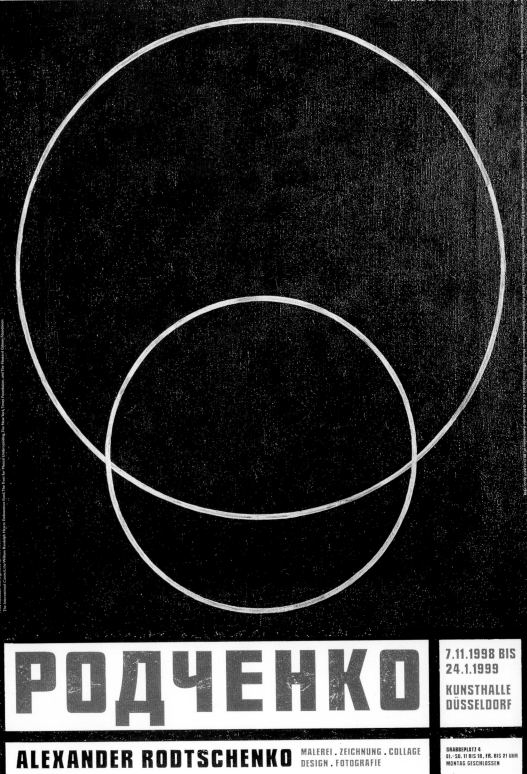

РОДЧЕНКО

**7.11.1998 BIS
24.1.1999**

**KUNSTHALLE
DÜSSELDORF**

ALEXANDER RODTSCHENKO

MALEREI . ZEICHNUNG . COLLAGE
DESIGN . FOTOGRAFIE

GRABBEPLATZ 4
DI.–SO. 11 BIS 18, FR. BIS 21 UHR
MONTAG GESCHLOSSEN

CAMPAIGN

Lettering
Helen Hacker

Art Direction
Helen Hacker
Düsseldorf, Germany

Creative Direction
Stefan Baggen

Account Managers
Sibylle Hinterwinkler and
Katja Sons

Design Office
Rempen & Partner: Das
Design Büro

Client
Kunsthalle Düsseldorf

Principal Type
Compacta, Gill Sans, and
custom type

Dimensions
Various

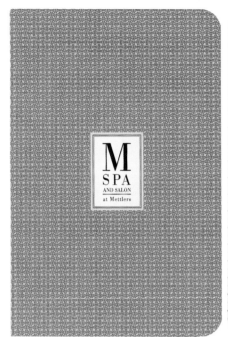

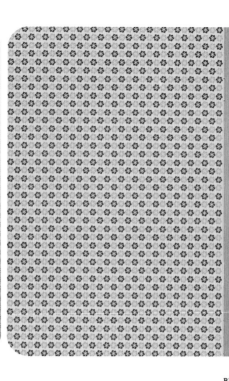

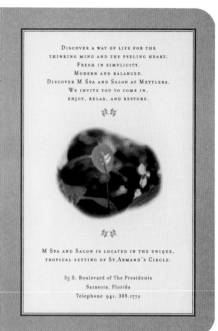

DISCOVER A WAY OF LIFE FOR THE
THINKING MIND AND THE FEELING HEART.
FRESH IN SIMPLICITY.
MODERN AND BALANCED.
DISCOVER M SPA AND SALON AT METTLERS.
WE INVITE YOU TO COME IN,
ENJOY, RELAX, AND RESTORE.

M SPA AND SALON IS LOCATED IN THE UNIQUE,
TROPICAL SETTING OF ST. ARMAND'S CIRCLE.

35 S. Boulevard of The Presidents
Sarasota, Florida
Telephone 941. 388.1772

BROCHURE
. . . .

Design
Giorgio Davanzo
Seattle, Washington
. . . .

Art Direction
Lanny French
. . . .

Agency
Foundation
. . . .

Client
M Spa
. . . .

Principal Type
Filosofia, Whirligig, and
Hypnopaedia
. . . .

Dimensions
5⅛ x 7½ in. (13 x 19.1 cm)

CAMPAIGN
· · · · · · · · · · · · · ·

Design
Efrat Rafaeli
Portland, Oregon
· · · · · · · · · · · · · ·

Art Direction
Efrat Rafaeli
· · · · · · · · · · · · · ·

Creative Direction
Eike Wintzer
· · · · · · · · · · · · · ·

Agency
ZIBA Design
· · · · · · · · · · · · · ·

Client
I.D.S.A.
· · · · · · · · · · · · · ·

Principal Type
Matrix family, Rotis Serif,
Centaur, and Garamond
· · · · · · · · · · · · · ·

Dimensions
Various

IDSA 1998 National Conference

WHY DESIGN?

NOT WHAT. NOT HOW. NOT WHEN.

BUT WHY? WHY DESIGN?

*SOME WILL ANSWER INSTANTLY.
OTHERS TAKE TIME TO PONDER.*

ONLY BY EXPLORING ALL THE ANSWERS CAN WE BEGIN
TO UNDERSTAND OUR STRENGTHS AND BUILD FOR A BETTER FUTURE.

PLEASE JOIN US FROM SEPTEMBER 23-26, FOR IDSA 1998 NATIONAL CONFERENCE
The Site: Hotel Del Coronado in San Diego, California

HOTEL DEL CORONADO
An Incomparable Site

Hotel Del Coronado is a beautifully restored, seaside resort, located along 33 oceanfront acres,
just ten minutes from downtown San Diego.

Built in 1887, the hotel has become a living legend with visits by thousands of celebrities and
dignitaries from around the world. Fourteen U.S. presidents have stayed at the hotel. Its most
famous visitor, then-Prince of Wales, met his future wife, Wallis Simpson, at the hotel in 1920.

The Del is also one of Hollywood's most popular filming locations. *Some Like It Hot,* starring
Marilyn Monroe, Jack Lemmon and Tony Curtis, was filmed at the Del as was the movie,
The Stunt Man, starring Peter O'Toole. Even the Emerald City, *The Wizard of Oz,* is said to be
based on the Del.

Located minutes from downtown San Diego, the Del is near such attractions as the San Diego
Zoo, Sea World, La Jolla, Disneyland, Mexico, Balboa Park and Old Town.

page [1]   Why Design? IDSA 1998 conference, hotel del coronado san diego, california

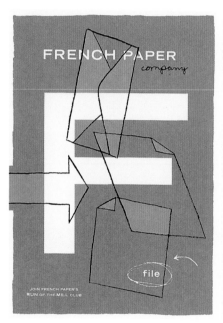
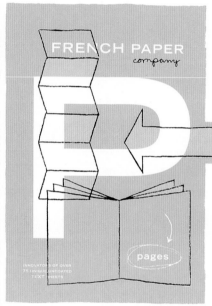
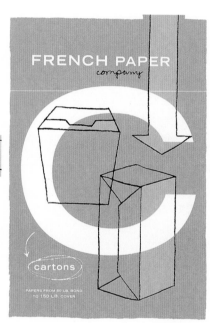

POSTCARDS

. . . .

Design
Jason Schulte
Minneapolis, Minnesota
. . . .

Art Direction
Charles S. Anderson
. . . .

Studio
Charles S. Anderson Design
. . . .

Client
French Paper Company
. . . .

Principal Type
Govern
. . . .

Dimensions
12¾ x 6 in. (32.4 x 15.2 cm)

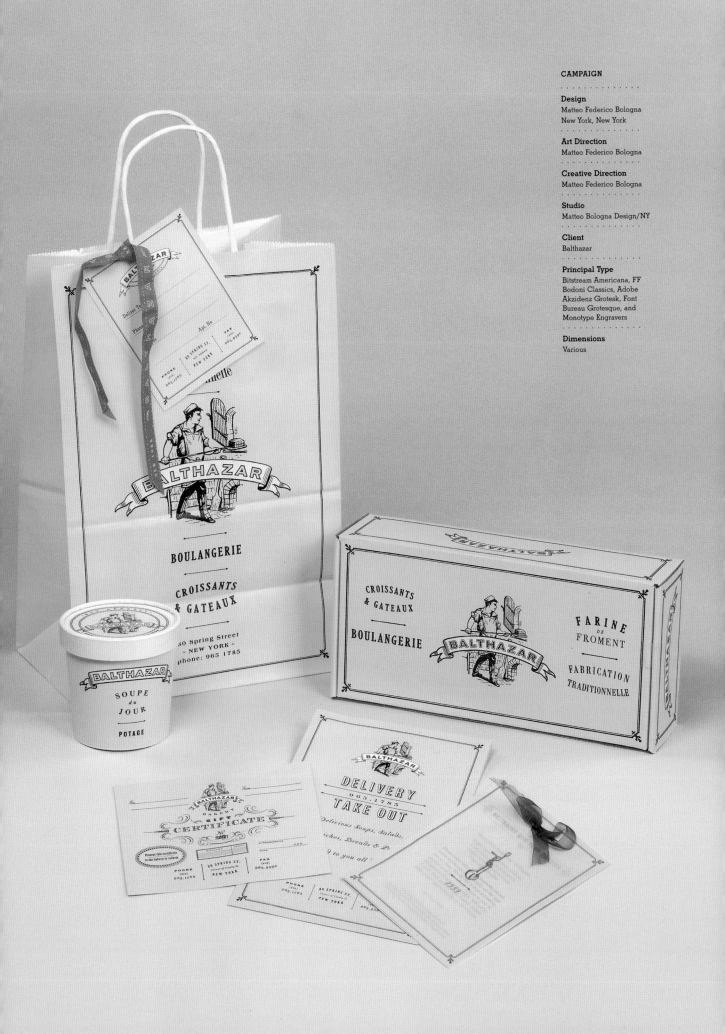

CAMPAIGN

Design
Matteo Federico Bologna
New York, New York

Art Direction
Matteo Federico Bologna

Creative Direction
Matteo Federico Bologna

Studio
Matteo Bologna Design/NY

Client
Balthazar

Principal Type
Bitstream Americana, FF
Bodoni Classics, Adobe
Akzidenz Grotesk, Font
Bureau Grotesque, and
Monotype Engravers

Dimensions
Various

SYRACUSE UNIVERSITY
PRESENTS

ALIVE!

GALLERY ★OF★ WEIRDOS

THE MODERN DOG

CIRCUS
SIDE SHOW

TRUE CONFESSIONS FROM DESIGN ADDICTS

MARCH 5

FIRST TIME HERE | **2 HEADS** | **FROM SEATTLE USA**

HAVE YOUR FORTUNE TOLD!

FABULOUS ODDITIES !
SHEMIN
AUDITORIUM

12:15 TO 1:45

VISUAL COMMUNICATIONS SYMPOSIUM

190 T D C 20

POSTER

Design
Robynne Raye
Seattle, Washington

Art Direction
Robynne Raye

Studio
Modern Dog

Client
Syracuse University

Principal Type
Barnum Block, Rodding,
various wood type

Dimensions
15 x 26 in. (38.1 x 66 cm)

Akademie Bildsprache

Anzeigen Trends·98

Semiotisches
Benchmarking

Semiotisches Benchmarking – Kommunikation auf dem Weg zum Erfolg.
Benchmarking ist ein Prozeß, eine Technik, die das Beobachten, Sammeln und
Analysieren von Fakten im Vergleich mit anderen meint. Benchmarking
beinhaltet, die eigene Leistung zu messen, Verbesserungen zu entwickeln und
Voraussetzungen für **Veränderungen** zu schaffen. Im Vergleich mit der
Konkurrenz, mit anderen Unternehmen und mit ähnlichen Produkten, zeigen sich
Lösungswege und Ziele, die in Strategien und Produktionsprozesse integriert
werden können. Da Benchmarking im Prozeß der kreativen Anzeigengestaltung
allerdings keine blanken Maßgaben, Fakten und Zahlen liefern kann, definieren
wir Semiotisches Benchmarking als Strategie, durch den Vergleich Kommunika-
tionstrends zu erkennen, zu deuten und zu entwickeln, mit denen sich Kommunikation wiederum einordnen, beurteilen und zielgerichtet verbessern läßt.
Die Ikonographie der Anzeigen'98 wirft Fragen auf: Welche visuellen und
verbalen Codes dominierten in den Motiven des Jahres? Welche gesellschafts-
relevanten Themen wurden angesprochen und verarbeitet? Wie nehmen
Marken und Unternehmen Bezug auf Veränderungen im Markt und in der Gesellschaft? Anzeigentrends.98 liefert keine Antworten, aber **Beobachtungen.**
Einen analytischen Blick auf die **Trends, Themen und Branchen** des Jahres, die
sich in den Anzeigen offensichtlich, versteckt oder getarnt präsentierten.

BROCHURE

Design
Régine Thienhaus
Hamburg, Germany

Lettering
Régine Thienhaus

Art Direction
Régine Thienhaus

Creative Direction
Professor Peter Wippermann

Publisher
Stefan Baumann

Editors
Dirk Nitschke and Dr. Immo
Wagner-Douglas

Agency
Büro Hamburg JK. PW.
Gesellschaft für
Kommunikationsdesign
GmbH

Client
Stiftung Akademie
Bildsprache gGmbH i.G.

Principal Type
Citizen

Dimensions
5 15/16 x 5 15/16 in. (15 x 15 cm)

VOL. 2 *No.* 1

THE **PANNUS** INDEX

8US$

3 EASY PIECES
Voices of the Pre-millennium

STEVEN TOMASULA   KEN G. YOUNG   HUGH FOX

BOOK COVER

· · · · · · · · · · · · ·

Design
Stephen Farrell
Chicago, Illinois
· · · · · · · · · · · · ·

Creative Direction
Stephen Farrell
· · · · · · · · · · · · ·

Studio
Slip Studios
· · · · · · · · · · · · ·

Client
The Pannus Index
· · · · · · · · · · · · ·

Principal Type
Barbera, Plastic Man, and
Grotesque MT
· · · · · · · · · · · · ·

Dimensions
10¼ x 6¾ in. (26 x 17.2 cm)

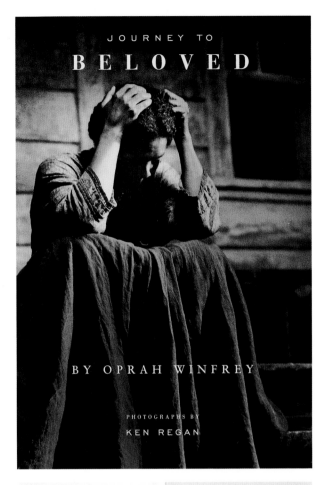

JOURNEY TO

BELOVED

BY OPRAH WINFREY

PHOTOGRAPHS BY
KEN REGAN

THE
STORY

HOW I FEEL ABOUT

BELOVED

[the book, the movie,
and the whole experience]

¶I am terribly insecure about my acting—
it's not something I do often enough to
know I do well. Jonathan has been so
helpful and encouraging, every day, every
scene. When Sethe is looking at Beloved's
shoes in the doorway and says, "Denver, is
she feverish?" JD tells me, "Really look
at the shoes." He says my nuances are
terrific. He says I have a gift. I'm not
certain. But I'm grateful he believes I do.
¶At the end of this week, we watched
Beloved breathe and be fed in dailies.
The scene—"you like shortenin' bread"—
featured beautiful Kimberly's bold eyes
and tentative excitement. Jonathan hugged
me and said many times over, "Thank you
for this wondrous experience." AMEN.

BOOK
· · · · · · · · · · · ·

Design
Emily Oberman and Bonnie
Siegler
New York, New York
· · · · · · · · · · · ·

Art Direction
Emily Oberman and Bonnie
Siegler
· · · · · · · · · · · ·

Creative Direction
Emily Oberman and Bonnie
Siegler
· · · · · · · · · · · ·

Photography
Ken Regan
· · · · · · · · · · · ·

Design Office
Number Seventeen
· · · · · · · · · · · ·

Client
Hyperion
· · · · · · · · · · · ·

Principal Type
Bodoni, Garamond, and
Sabon
· · · · · · · · · · · ·

Dimensions
9¼ x 12¼ in. (23.5 x
31.1 cm)

CAMP HEARTLAND

One Big Heart

FIRST DAY OF CAMP

Willow River, Minnesota

JUNE TWENTY-SIXTH NINETEEN NINETY-EIGHT

CAMPAIGN
. . . .

Design
Alan Colvin and Sida
Phungjiam
Minneapolis, Minnesota
. . . .

Art Direction
Alan Colvin
. . . .

Creative Direction
Joe Duffy
. . . .

Design Office
Duffy Design and Interactive
. . . .

Client
Camp Heartland
. . . .

Principal Type
Bulldog, Champion Gothic,
Franklin Gothic, Standard,
and Trade Gothic
. . . .

Dimensions
Various

◄

CAMPAIGN
. . . .

Design
Scott Rier and Samuel
G. Shelton
Washington, D.C.
. . . .

Art Direction
Samuel G. Shelton and
Laura Latham
. . . .

Copywriter
Heather and Matt Philbin,
Laura Latham, and Samuel
G. Shelton
Alexandria, Virginia and
Washington, D.C.
. . . .

Studio
KINETIK Communication
Graphics
. . . .

Client
American Institute of
Graphic Arts/
Washington, D.C.
. . . .

Principal Type
Base 9 and Clarendon
. . . .

Dimensions
Various

★ STRIPPER
LESSONS

BY: JOHN
O'BRIEN

★ BY THE AUTHOR OF: "LEAVING LAS VEGAS"

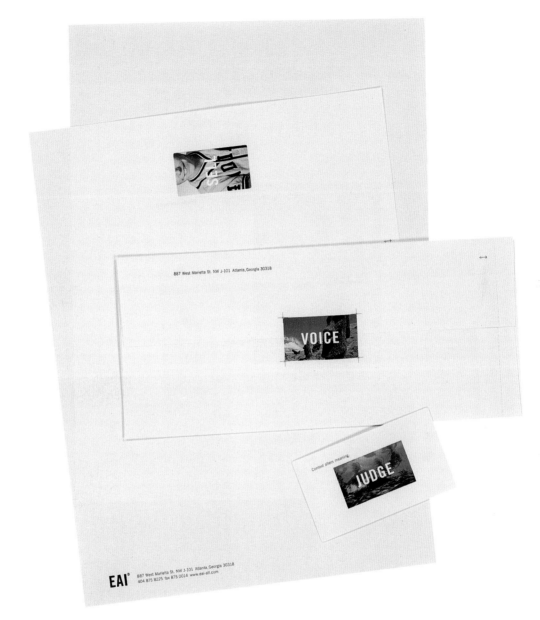

◄

MAGAZINE

· · · · · · · · · · · · ·

Design
Wang Xu
Guangzhou, China

· · · · · · · · · · · · ·

Art Direction
Wang Xu

· · · · · · · · · · · · ·

Creative Direction
Wang Xu

· · · · · · · · · · · · ·

Studio
Wang Xu & Associates Ltd.

· · · · · · · · · · · · ·

Client
China Youth Press

· · · · · · · · · · · · ·

Principal Type
Myriad MM

· · · · · · · · · · · · ·

Dimensions
11 x 14¾ in. (28 x 37.5 cm)

Graphic Design
in the Netherlands
How a little country
can still be big

ANNUAL REPORT

Design
Marion English
Birmingham, Alabama

Art Direction
Marion English

Creative Direction
Marion English

Photography
Don Harbor and Fredik Broden

Agency
Slaughter Hanson

Client
Greater Alabama Council of the Boy Scouts of America

Principal Type
Bell Gothic and Venetian

Dimensions
9 x 12 in. (22.9 x 30.5 cm)

BROCHURE
. . . .

Design
Paula Scher, Anke
Stohlmann, and Keith Daigle
New York, New York
. . . .

Art Direction
Paula Scher
. . . .

Studio
Pentagram Design
. . . .

Client
Mohawk Paper Mills
. . . .

Principal Type
Franklin Gothic Extra
Condensed
. . . .

Dimensions
11 x 11½ in. (27.9 x 29.2 cm)

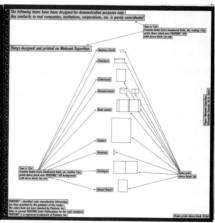

POSTER
. . . .

Design
Bob van Dijk
The Hague, The Netherlands
. . . .

Lettering
Bob van Dijk
. . . .

Photography
Deen van Meer
Amsterdam, The Netherlands
. . . .

Studio
Studio Dumbar
. . . .

Client
The Holland Dance Festival
. . . .

Principal Type
News Gothic and
handlettering
. . . .

Dimensions
Various

▶

the hague

holland
dance
festival

4-21 february '98

the dancer's tale

4-21 February 1998

LUCENT DANSTHEATER
Sylvie Guillem (International) **4, 5**
The Dancer's Destiny Gala (NL) **6**
    NDT I, II, III
Nederlands Dans Theater II (NL) **7, 8**
Nederlands Dans Theater I (NL) **11, 12**
Tanztheater der Komischen Oper, Berlin (D) **13, 14**
Compañía Nacional de Danza (E) **17, 18**
Nederlands Dans Theater III (NL) **20, 21**

THEATER AAN HET SPUI
Rennie Harris Pure Movement, Hiphop (USA) **5, 6**
Galili Dance (NL) **8, 9**
Speelteater Gent (B) **11**
Richard Alston Dance Company (GB) **12, 13**
Batsheva Ensemble / The Junior Company (IL) **14, 15**
A Dancer's Tale, Spui (International) **17, 18**
    Dansers uit alle windstreken
Dansgroep De Meekers (NL) **18**
Grip: Mathilde Santing en Anne Affourtit (NL) **19, 20, 21**
Gayle Tufts en Rainer Bielfeldt (D) **12, 13, 14**
    Late night cabaret

KORZO THEATER
Ocho, Tango (NL) **6, 7**
A Taste of Glamour, Eigentijdse Dansopera (NL) **9, 10**
A Dancer's Tale, Korzo (International) **12, 13, 14**
    Dansers uit alle windstreken
Piet Rogie/Compagnie Peter Bulcaen (NL) **17, 18**
A Fleur de Peau (F) **20, 21**

KONINKLIJK CONSERVATORIUM
Dansacademies (NL, GB) **6, 7, 8**
    Den Haag, Rotterdam, Amsterdam, Londen

INTERNATIONAL SYMPOSIUM
The Dancer of the XXI Century **6, 7, 8**
Education for Transition in a Changing World

FESTIVALKASSA (070) 360 49 30

PACKAGING

· · · · · · · · · · · · · ·

Design
Matti Cross
Vancouver, British Columbia,
Canada

· · · · · · · · · · · · · ·

Art Direction
Matti Cross

· · · · · · · · · · · · · ·

Creative Direction
Ken Koo

· · · · · · · · · · · · · ·

Photography
Clinton Hussey

· · · · · · · · · · · · · ·

Agency
Koo Creative Group

· · · · · · · · · · · · · ·

Client
Metropolitan Hotels
"Sen5es"

· · · · · · · · · · · · · ·

Principal Type
Univers and Carmella

· · · · · · · · · · · · · ·

Dimensions
Various

1997 ANNUAL REPORT, DOW JONES & COMPANY

ANNUAL REPORT
. . . .

Design
Craig Williamson and Thai
Nguyen
New York, New York

Art Direction
Hans Neubert

Creative Direction
Howard Belk
. . . .

Agency
Belk Mignogna Associates

Client
Dow Jones & Company
. . . .

Principal Type
Adobe Trade Gothic and
various Wall St. Journal
typefaces
. . . .

Dimensions
9 x 11¾ in. (22.9 x 30 cm)

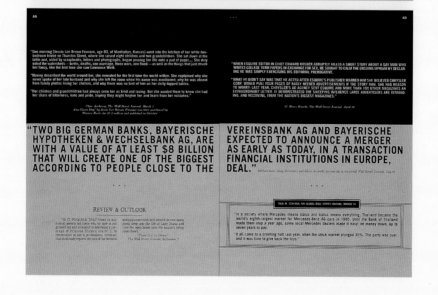

IT'S TIME TO HAVE ONE WITH THE NEIGHBORS!

IT'S MILLER TIME.

IT'S TIME FOR BEER D'OEUVRES.

IT'S MGD MILLER TIME.

▲

POINT OF PURCHASE
. . . .
Design
Heath Lowe and Joe Peila
Portland, Oregon
. . . .
Art Direction
Alicia Johnson and Hal
Wolverton
. . . .
Creative Direction
Alicia Johnson and Hal
Wolverton
. . . .
Photography
Melody McDaniel
Los Angeles, California
. . . .
Illustration
Rob and Christian Clayton
Los Angeles, California
. . . .
Agency
Wieden & Kennedy
. . . .
Studio
Johnson & Wolverton
. . . .
Client
Miller Brewing Co.
. . . .
Principal Type
Interstate
. . . .
Dimensions
12 x 14 in. (30.5 x 35.6 cm)

. . . .
PACKAGING
. . . .
Design
Starlee Matz
Portland, Oregon
. . . .
Art Direction
Steve Sandstrom
. . . .
Creative Direction
Steve Sandstrom
. . . .
Copywriter
Buddy T. Ramstedder and
Steve Sandstrom
. . . .
Studio
Sandstrom Design
. . . .
Client
Miller Brewing Co.
. . . .
Principal Type
Franklin Gothic, Alternate
Gothic, Snell Roundhand,
ITC Officina, Helvetica,
Kuenstler, and Engravers
Gothic

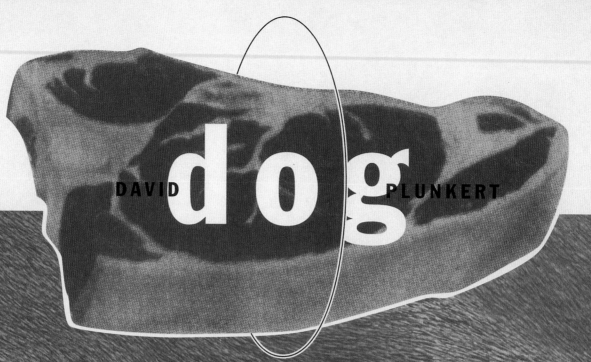

DAVID **dog** PLUNKERT

&

AIGA | **SPUR**
american institute of graphic arts | human tools of capitalism

JOYCE **pony** HESSELBERTH

n Evening of Artfully Artless Graphic Design. Wed 23 Sept @ 6:00pm. Price per lb/FREE
race Street Theatre. 934 West Grace Street, Richmond VA
ponsored by AIGA Richmond & VCU Communication Arts & Design
or more information call 804 262 8383

show

POSTER

Design
David Plunkert
Baltimore, Maryland

Art Direction
David Plunkert

Design Office
Spur Design LLC

Client
American Institute of
Graphic Arts/Richmond

Principal Type
Franklin Gothic Condensed

Dimensions
18 x 24.5 in. (45.7 x 62.2 cm)

LOGOTYPE

Design
Vittorio Costarella
Seattle, Washington

Art Direction
Vittorio Costarella

Creative Direction
Carmen, Pete, and Rosie

Studio
Modern Dog

Principal Type
Helvetica Neue Extended

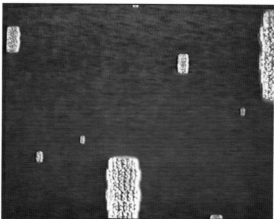

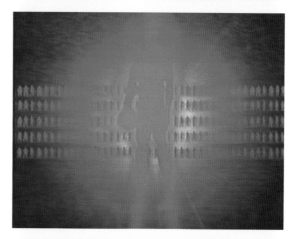

POSTER

. . . .

Design
Minza Tsukada
Tokyo, Japan

. . . .

Art Direction
Minza Tsukada

. . . .

Photography
Toshinobu Kobayashi

. . . .

Studio
Strike Co., Ltd.

. . . .

Principal Type
KG-A and BT-A

. . . .

Dimensions
40⁹/₁₆ x 28⁵/₈ in. (103 x
72.8 cm)

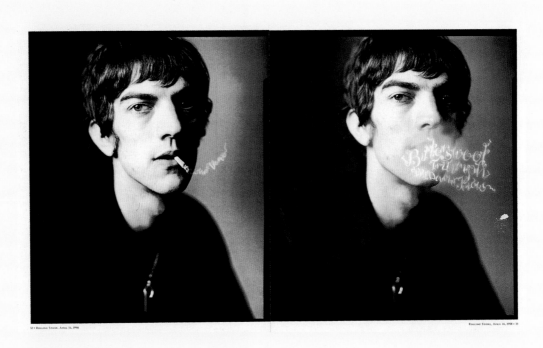

MAGAZINE SPREAD

. . . .

Design
Fred Woodward and Gail
Anderson
New York, New York

. . . .

Art Direction
Fred Woodward

. . . .

Photography
Mark Seliger

. . . .

Photo Editor
Rachel Knepfer

. . . .

Client
Rolling Stone

. . . .

Principal Type
Housemaid

. . . .

Dimensions
12 x 20 in. (30.5 x 50.8 cm)

汗をタオルで拭く間に、おいしいむぎ茶が出来てますよ。

MAGAZINE SPREAD

Design
D. J. Stout and Nancy
McMillen
Austin, Texas

Lettering
D. J. Stout

Art Direction
D. J. Stout

Creative Direction
D. J. Stout

Studio
TexasMonthly

Principal Type
Handlettering

Dimensions
11 x 17 in. (27.9 x 43.2 cm)

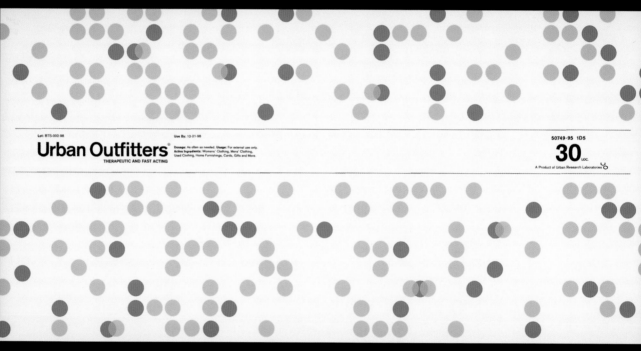

CAMPAIGN

Design
Jeremy Dean and Lance
Rusoff
Philadelphia, Pennsylvania

Art Direction
Lance Rusoff

Creative Direction
Sue Otto

Agency
Urban Outfitters

Principal Type
Akzidenz Grotesk

Dimensions
Various

There's Something about Weeping Mary

Images of a tiny CHEROKEE COUNTY community capture a forgotten corner of TEXAS' RURAL PAST.

"THE NAME WAS WHAT ATTRACTED ME FIRST," PHOTOGRAPHER O. RUFUS LOVETT says of Weeping Mary, a Cherokee County hamlet that he has chronicled over the past four years. Settled shortly after the Civil War by liberated slaves from nearby plantations, the community may have been named for Mary Magdalene or the Virgin Mary, but local folklore identifies the Mary in question as a freedwoman who was tricked out of her land by a rich white man.

When Lovett set out to find the isolated community, it didn't even rate a highway sign. "When I first visited, early on, there may have been some suspicion," says Lovett, a Longview resident who is a photography instructor at Kilgore College, "but everyone welcomed me. When I told them I'd like to take some pictures, they invited me back, and

Photographs by O. RUFUS LOVETT

after I photographed them and gave them photographs to keep, we became friends."

That kindness, Lovett says, is Weeping Mary's greatest charm. "It's the kind of place where everybody takes care of one another. Kids are looked after by parents, uncles, aunts, cousins, neighbors, church ladies. Everyone attends everything. Last time I was out there, it was the bonfire and wienie roast at Brother Parker's—he's the deacon at the Baptist church." Except for a solitary fix-it shop, Weeping Mary has no businesses. Some residents are loggers or farmers; others work for the highway department or the state hospital in Rusk, eighteen miles away. A lack of jobs may keep Weeping Mary small—its population, though not officially recorded, is around two hundred—but Lovett is sure it will endure. "Some people have moved away," he says, "but most people grew up there and now are raising their own children in Weeping Mary. They have a lot to be proud of." ANNE DINGUS

CLOTHESPINS LINE "This was on EASTER SUNDAY, a nice East Texas Spring day. I was just walking around the neighborhood and noticed some CHILDREN playing and the Rhythm of the CLOTHESPINS matched the Rhythm of the TRAMPOLINE the KIDS bouncing on."

TWO BROTHERS 1996 "I call these TWO KIDS 'THE SWIMMERS.' They were in their UNDERPANTS because they'd been SWIMMING in a little plastic POOL in their BACK YARD."

UNCLE BILL 1998 He's the oldest person in WEEPING MARY, 93 years old. Sort of the Village Elder. He's on his front PORCH, Just sitting on the steps, enjoying the day."

Chi Chi's Cousin 1995 "I had just made a PICTURE of something else in a different direction when I felt someone else's presence and I saw this little GIRL watching ME. I just FASCINATED. I just PIVOTED and took her PICTURE."

DEMITRIA'S SHOES 1995 "I took this PICTURE right after church. I loved her Sunday Socks and her Sunday Shoes."

Mama's Dress 1994 "This was one of the WOMEN at THE POPE FAMILY REUNION preparing to serve the FOOD. The patterned DRESS is reminiscent of a FLOWERED DRESS of my Mother's that I would cling to as a child."

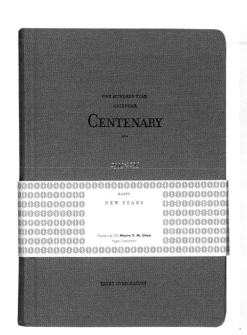

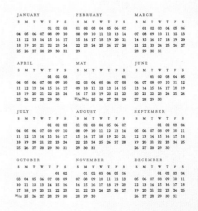

THE YEAR

TWO THOUSAND

and

SIXTY

2060

remarks

CALENDAR

. . . .

Design
Pacey Chao
Taipei, Taiwan

. . . .

Creative Direction
Van So

. . . .

Copywriters
Brent Heinrich and R. V.
Dougherty

. . . .

Production
China Blue

. . . .

Agency
JRV International Company

. . . .

Client
Yageo Corporation

. . . .

Principal Type
Filosofia

. . . .

Dimensions
5⅛ x 7³/₁₆ in. (13 x 18.2 cm)

BROCHURE

. . . .

Creative Direction
Andreas Uebele
Stuttgart, Germany

. . . .

Drawings
Arnold Walz

. . . .

Studio
Büro Uebele Visuelle
Kommunikation

. . . .

Client
Rosso Objekte Nimbus
GmbH

. . . .

Principal Type
Serifa Light

. . . .

Dimensions
5⅛ x 6¹¹/₁₆ in. (13 x
17 cm)

September

99

August 99

1	2	3	4	5	6	7
8	9	10	11	12	13	14
15	16	17	18	19	20	21
22	23	24	25	26	27	28
29	30	31				

October 99

					1	2
3	4	5	6	7	8	9
10	11	12	13	14	15	16
17	18	19	20	21	22	23
24	25	26	27	28	29	30
31						

sun	mon	tue	wed	thu	fri	sat
			1	2	3	4
5	6	7	8	9	10	11
12	13	14	15	16	17	18
19	20	21	22	23	24	25
26	27	28	29	30		

**Offer #9
MonoCable**
One month free service*

MonoCable is a one-channel specialty channel for jaded media consumers who believe choice is over-rated and exhausting. With MonoCable, you get one channel, all the time, with no programming, no hassles with your spouse over control of the remote and, best of all, it's available at one-tenth the cost of the average cable service. When you're bored with a universe of televisual media at your fingertips, try nothing instead!

COMING THIS MONTH ON MONOCABLE!
Test patterns of the 50s, 60s, and 70s!

*MONOCABLE IS A BUNDLED SERVICE AVAILABLE WITHIN THE GALACTIC SPECIALTY PACKAGE COMPRISING 3,123 CABLE CHANNELS AND 100,007 MULTIMEDIA WEBSITES. BASIC ANNUAL SUBSCRIPTION AT $1,499.11 (NOT INCLUDING COMPULSORY NETWORK EXPANSION BILLING).

Concrete
DESIGN COMMUNICATIONS INC. SERVING DISCERNING BUYERS OF DESIGN FOR OVER A DECADE
416-534-9960

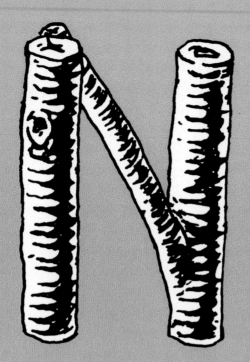
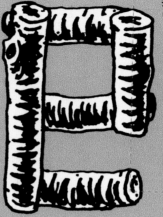

**MOVING
ANNOUNCEMENT**
· · · · · · · · · · · · ·

Design
James Victore
Beacon, New York
· · · · · · · · · · · · ·

Lettering
James Victore
· · · · · · · · · · · · ·

Agency
James Victore, Inc.
· · · · · · · · · · · · ·

Principal Type
Chicago and wood type
· · · · · · · · · · · · ·

Dimensions
5 x 7 in. (12.7 x 17.8 cm)

7431 Covington Highway *Lithonia, Ga.* 30058
Telephone 770~482~5100 • Facsimile 770~484~1304

STATIONERY

Design
Philip Shore
Atlanta, Georgia

Lettering
Philip Shore

Art Direction
Edward Jett

Creative Direction
Edward Jett

Production
Heath Beeferman

Studio
Deep Design

Client
Dr. Michael Smith's
Veterinary Collectibles

Principal Type
Stone Serif, Engravure, Snell,
and Campanile

Dimensions
8½ x 11 in. (21.6 x 27.9 cm)

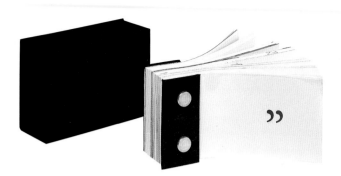

STUDENT WORK

. . . .

Design
Fredrik Bladh
San Francisco, California

. . . .

Instructor
Suzanne West

. . . .

School
Academy of Art College

. . . .

Principal Type
Various

. . . .

Dimensions
4³⁄₄ x 2¹⁄₂ in. (12.1 x
6.4 cm)

MAGAZINE SPREAD

. . . .

Design
Tom Brown and Rob Hewitt
Coquitlam, British Columbia,
Canada

. . . .

Art Direction
Tom Brown

. . . .

Creative Direction
Sarah Vinas
New York, New York

. . . .

Agency
Deloitte & Touche

. . . .

Principal Type
Interstate and Electra

. . . .

Dimensions
12 x 17 in. (30.5 x 43.2 cm)

pension reform worth the gamble

privatization could be a smart bet—or a one-way ticket to palookaville.
BY VANESSA DRUCKER
ILLUSTRATIONS BY BRIAN CRONIN

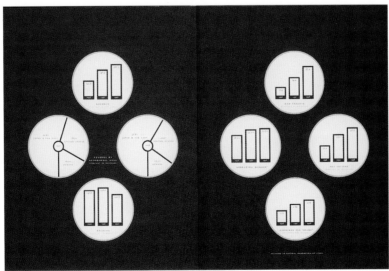

ANNUAL REPORT
. . . .
Design
Lian Ng
San Francisco, California
. . . .
Art Direction
Bill Cahan
. . . .
Creative Direction
Bill Cahan
. . . .
Agency
Cahan & Associates
. . . .
Client
Etec Systems
. . . .
Principal Type
Bembo and Trade Gothic
. . . .
Dimensions
9 x 11½ in. (22.9 x 29.2 cm)

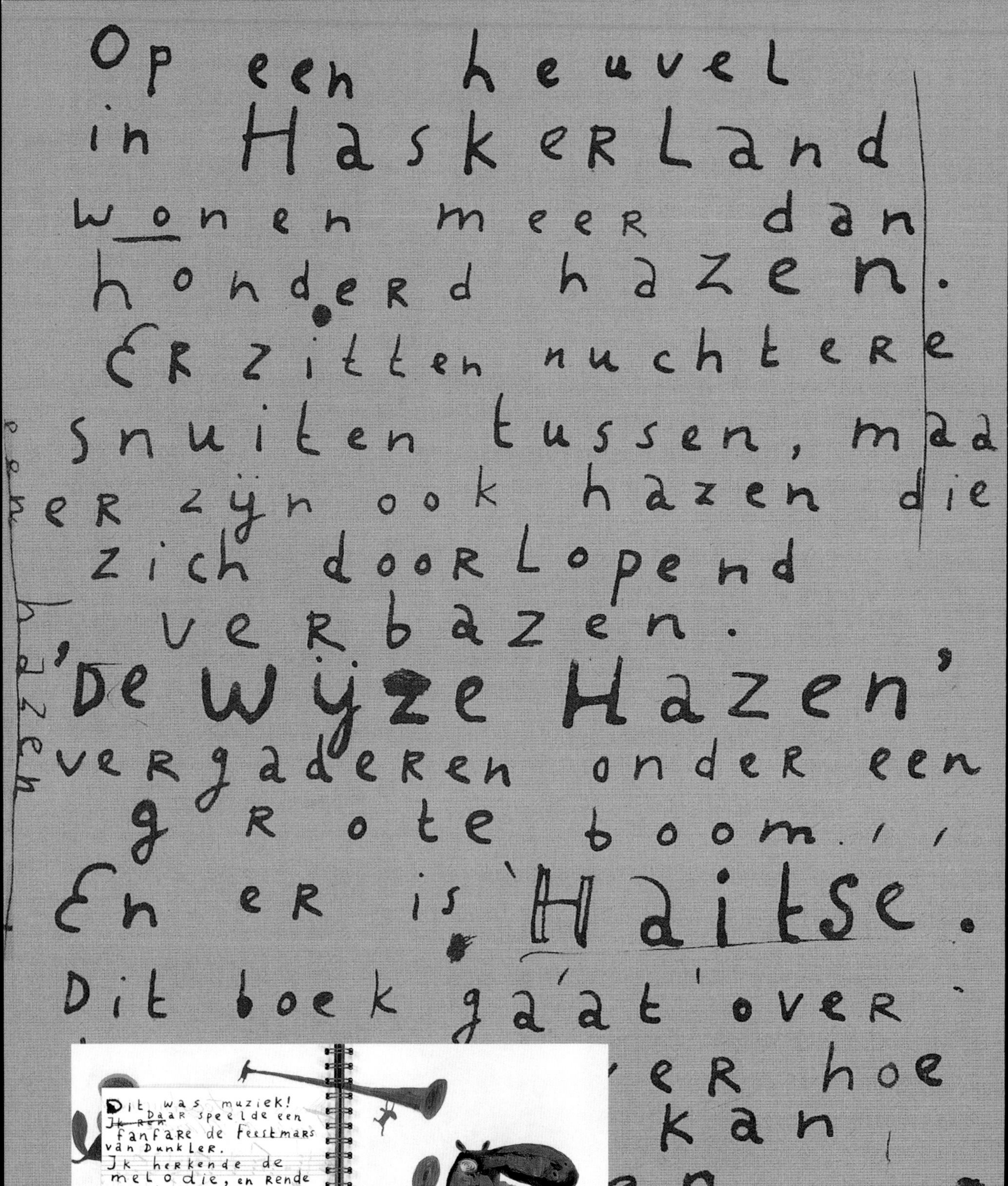

Op een heuvel
in Haskerland
wonen meer dan
honderd hazen.
Er zitten nuchtere
snuiten tussen, maa
er zijn ook hazen die
zich doorlopend
verbazen.
'De Wijze Hazen'
vergaderen onder een
grote boom.//
En er is 'Haitse.
Dit boek gaat over
er hoe
kan
en...

BOOK

. . . .

Design
Richard van der Horst
Amsterdam, The Netherlands

. . . .

Calligraphy
Bart van Leeuwen

. . . .

Art Direction
André Toet

. . . .

Creative Direction
André Toet

. . . .

Illustration
Bart van Leeuwen

. . . .

Design Office
Samenwerkende Ontwerpers

. . . .

Client
Haskerland bv

. . . .

Principal Type
Handlettering

. . . .

Dimensions
10¼ x 11⁷/₁₆ in. (26 x
29.5 cm)

◄

POSTER

. . . .

Design
Petra Janssen and Edwin
Vollebergh
's-Hertogenbosch,
The Netherlands

. . . .

Lettering
Petra Janssen and Edwin
Vollebergh

. . . .

Art Direction
Petra Janssen and Edwin
Vollebergh

. . . .

Creative Direction
Petra Janssen and Edwin
Vollebergh

. . . .

Printer
Kerlensky Zeefdruk
Boxel, The Netherlands

. . . .

Studio
Studio Boot

. . . .

Principal Type
Tiger

. . . .

Dimensions
32¹¹/₁₆ x 23⁷/₁₆ in. (83 x
59.5 cm)

roger:bl@ck

sig: up and UNITED DIGITAL ARTISTS present: Voice and Vision on the Web: An Evening with Roger Black. A 1999 sig: up / USA New Media Design Lecture.

Wednesday, January 13, 1999, 7pm. Great Hall / Cooper Union / 7 East 7th Street (NYC) AIGA/NY members $10. Non-members $25. Students with valid ID $6. Students with valid ID Free

(r)evolution: for his magazine / newspaper design, Roger Black, author of the best-selling book "Web Sites That Work," has put himself at the forefront of talent design with ground-breaking work on / remix. Discovery Channel Online, and many other Web sites. Roger's design principles and methodology are informed by the outstanding editorial design that his reputation is built upon.

(r)emake: Roger will discuss how to create an engaging vision while making an emotional and visual impact on the Web. This event is part of the sig: up/USA New Media Design Series.

See the book for more info, and some great deals. Exclusive pre-event ID. has been generously provided by Cornell Printing Company.

POSTER
· · · · · · · · · · · · ·
Design
John Klotnia
New York, New York
· · · · · · · · · · · · ·
Client
American Institute of
Graphic Arts/New York
· · · · · · · · · · · · ·
Principal Type
Egiziano
· · · · · · · · · · · · ·
Dimensions
24 x 36 in. (61 x 91.4 cm)

◀

FILM TITLES
· · · · · · · · · · · · ·
Design
Jim Kenney, Adam Bluming,
Kyle Cooper, and Michael
Riley
Los Angeles, California
· · · · · · · · · · · · ·
Art Direction
Michael Riley
· · · · · · · · · · · · ·
Creative Direction
Kyle Cooper
· · · · · · · · · · · · ·
Executive Producer
Peter Frankfurt
· · · · · · · · · · · · ·
Producer
Tim Thompson
· · · · · · · · · · · · ·
Studio
Imaginary Forces
· · · · · · · · · · · · ·
Client
DreamWorks SKG
· · · · · · · · · · · · ·
Principal Type
Granjon Bold

Roberto de Vicq
de Cumptich
New York, New York
. . . .

Creative Direction
Roberto de Vicq
de Cumptich
. . . .

Client
Broadway Books
. . . .

Principal Type
Base 9, Bovine Poster, and
Amazone
. . . .

Dimensions
6⅛ x 9¼ in. (15.6 x 23.5 cm)

COOKBOOK

HEY THERE, CHILI NATION:
TIME TO CHOW DOWN AND CHILI UP!

Here is the most comprehensive guide ever to making and enjoying America's favorite meal in a bowl.

From California's Gilroy Super Garlic Chili and Florida's Havana Moon Chili to Wisconsin's Green Bay Chili and New Hampshire's Yankee Bean Pot Chili, *Chili Nation* features chili recipes from all fifty states. With their incomparable wit and style, Jane and Michael Stern offer chili history and trivia, a mail-order guide to the best spices and peppers, and tales of beloved chili parlors coast to coast.

Praise for JANE AND MICHAEL STERN

"Jane and Michael Stern . . . should be given a medal and then promptly sent off to donut rehab." —*Time Out New York*

Praise for *Eat Your Way Across the U.S.A.*

"Jane and Michael Stern's *Eat Your Way Across the U.S.A.* offers rhapsodic celebrations of American regional food." —*New York* magazine

"The Sterns have compiled a cross-country culinary guide that should be stashed in every food lover's glove compartment, right next to the maps and the Swiss Army knife. . . . [This book] sure does make you want to head out to the back roads and blue highways and chow down." —*People* magazine

Jane and Michael Stern are the authors of more than twenty books about America, including *Eat Your Way Across the U.S.A.* and *Roadfood*. They write the "Two for the Road" column in *Gourmet* and the "Wish You Were Here" postcards for Condé Nast's *Epicurious* on the World Wide Web. The Sterns, who are regular contributors to Public Radio's *The Splendid Table*, have also written for *The New Yorker* and made frequent appearances on CBS *This Morning* and NBC's *Saturday Today*. They live in Connecticut.

US $12.00 / $19.00 CAN

ISBN 0-7679-0263-7

51200

COVER DESIGN BY
Roberto de Vicq
de Cumptich

B BROADWAY

9 780767 902632

CHILI NATION ✪ *Jane & Michael Stern*

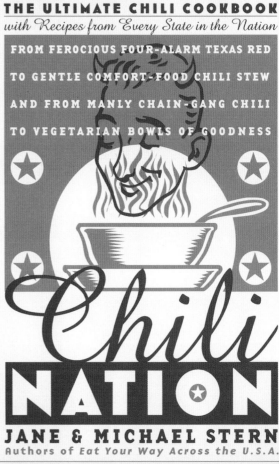

✪

THE ULTIMATE CHILI COOKBOOK
with Recipes from Every State in the Nation

FROM FEROCIOUS FOUR-ALARM TEXAS RED
TO GENTLE COMFORT-FOOD CHILI STEW
AND FROM MANLY CHAIN-GANG CHILI
TO VEGETARIAN BOWLS OF GOODNESS

Chili
NATION

JANE & MICHAEL STERN
Authors of *Eat Your Way Across the U.S.A.*

B BROADWAY

PACKAGING

. . . .

Design
Anka Kammler and Ludwig
Spormann
Berlin, Germany

. . . .

Studio
zeer fijn

. . . .

Client
Insolito Records

. . . .

Principal Type
Various

. . . .

Dimensions
7¼ x 7 in. (18.5 x 18 cm)

PROMOTION

. . . .

Design
Philip Krayna
San Francisco, California

. . . .

Lettering
Philip Krayna

. . . .

Studio
Philip Krayna Design

. . . .

Principal Type
Weiss and handlettering

. . . .

Dimensions
8 x 6 in. (20.3 x 15.2 cm)

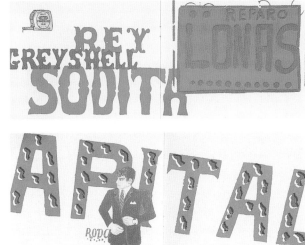

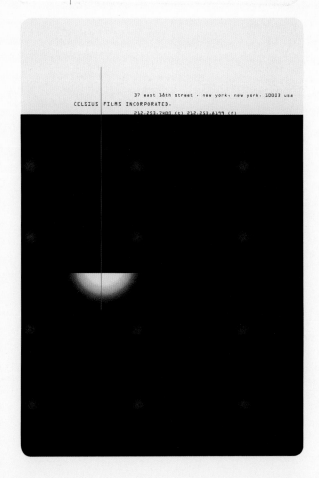

STATIONERY

· · · · · · · · · · · · ·

Design
Carlos Segura
Chicago, Illinois
· · · · · · · · · · · · ·

Lettering
Carlos Segura
· · · · · · · · · · · · ·

Art Direction
Carlos Segura
· · · · · · · · · · · · ·

Creative Direction
Carlos Segura
· · · · · · · · · · · · ·

Design Office
Segura, Inc.
· · · · · · · · · · · · ·

Client
Celsius Films
· · · · · · · · · · · · ·

Principal Type
OCR-B
· · · · · · · · · · · · ·

Dimensions
8½ x 11 in. (21.6 x 27.9 cm)

INTE·GRAL, ADJ. 1. NEEDED FOR COMPLETENESS: ESSENTIAL FOR THE WHOLE. AS AN INTEGRAL PART. 2. COMPOSED OF PARTS THAT MAKE ONE UNITED WHOLE. AS AN INTEGRAL WHOLE. 3. LACKING NOTHING ESSENTIAL TO COMPLETENESS: ENTIRE. 4. MATH. OF BEING, OR RELATING TO, AN INTEGER, NOT FRACTIONAL. – N. A WHOLE. A WHOLE NUMBER: IN·TEGRAL. ADJ. 1. NECESSARY FOR COMPLETENESS: THE ARMS AND LEGS ARE – (BUT NOT ESSENTIAL) PARTS OF A HUMAN BEING. 2. WHOLE; HAV- ING OR CONTAINING ALL PARTS THAT ARE NECESSARY FOR COMPLETENESS. 3. [MATH] OF, DENOTED BY, AN INTEGER; MADE UP OF INTEGERS. – CF ADV./IN·TE· GRAL SCIENCES. A KEY PROJECT IN THE FIELD OF GAMMA-RAY ASTRONOMY AND HIGH ENERGY ASTROPHYSICS OF THE NEXT DECADE, INTEGRAL IS DEDICATED TO FINE GAMMA-RAY SPECTROSCOPY [E-]IMAGE] = 500] AND ACCURATE IMAGING OF CELESTIAL SOURCES IN THE ENERGY BAND 15 KEV TO 10 MEV WITH CONCURRENT SOURCE MONITORING IN THE X-RAY [3-35 KEV] AND OPTICAL (V-BAND, 550 NM) BANDS. INTEGRAL WILL BE LIFTED ON INTO A HIGH APOGEE ORBIT BY THE RUS- SIAN PROTON LAUNCHER IN 2001. —RUSSIAN SCIENCE DATA CENTER FOR INTE- GRAL [RSDC] [IMAGE] PARTICIPATION OF RUSSIA IN THE PROJECT [IMAGE] AIMS AND SCOPE OF RUSSIAN SCIENCE DATA CENTER [IMAGE] RUSSIAN TIME ALLOCA- TION COMMITTEE RELATED LINKS. [IMAGE] INTEGRAL PROJECT AT ESTEC [IMAGE] INTEGRAL SCIENCE DATA CENTER AT GENEVA [IMAGE] SPACE RESEARCH INSTITUTE [IKI] AT MOSCOW [IMAGE] HIGH ENERGY ASTROPHYSICS IN IKI [IMAGE] THE 3RD IN- TEGRAL WORKSHOP "THE EXTREME UNIVERSE" IN·TE·I GRAL. 1. EIN GANZES AUS- MACHEND; GANZ, VOLLSTÄNDIG. II INTEGRIEREND, WESENTLICH [– DAS; -S, -E

[MATH] RECHENSYMBOL DER INTEGRALRECHNUNG, ZEICHEN: ∫ 2. MATHEMATI- SCHER SUMMENAUSDRUCK ÜBER DIE DIFFERENTIALE EINES ENDLICHEN OD UN- ENDLICHEN BEREICHS! INTE·I GRAL [MLAT. =EIN GANZES AUSMACHEND]. ZU LAT. INTEGRARE =WIEDERHERSTELLEN]. <ERGÄNZEN!] DAS; -S,-E. ANALYSIS: 1) GRUNDBEGRIFF DER – INTEGRALRECHNUNG. 2) [BEZ FÜR DIE LÖSUNG EINER – DIF- FERENTIALGLEICHUNG]! INTEGRAL I EXPONENTIELLE DIE DURCH DIE INTEGRAL- DARSTELLUNG [..] DEFINIERTE FUNKTION FÜR KOMPLEXEN VERÄNDERLICHEN.– SIE BESITZT DIE REIHENENTWICKLUNG [..] WOBEI C DIE EULERSCHE KONSTANTE IST.! IN·I TE·I GRAL, DAS; -S, -E [MATH] RECHENSYMBOL DER INTEGRALRECHNUNG, ZEI- CHEN: ∫ 2. MATHEMATISCHER SUMMENAUSDRUCK ÜBER DIE DIFFERENTIALE EINES ENDLICHEN OD. UNENDLICHEN BEREICHS! INTEGRALE STRUKTUR: "ABER NICHT ALLE FOLGTEN. NICHT ALLE WOLLKTER IN DIE VON DESCARTES POSTULIERTE TRENNUNG, IN DIESE RATIONALE TEILUNG DESSEN EIN, WAS UNVERWANDT ZUSAMMENGEHÖRT: MENTALES UND MATERIE. DIES IST DAS ENTSCHEIDENDE, UND ZWAR IST ES ENTSCHEIDEND FÜR DIE MANIFESTATIONEN EINER NEUEN BE- WUSSTSEINSSTRUKTUR. SIE SIND DAS ANZEICHEN DAFÜR, DASS SICH IM MEN- SCHEN JENE BEWUSSTSEINS-MUTATION VOLLZIEHT, AUS DER HERAUS SICH PERSPEKTIVISCHE WELT GESTALTEN MAG. IN·I TE·I GRAL, VON LEIBNIZ EINGEF. ZUR BEZ. DES GEGENBEGRIFFS ZU" DIFFERENTIAL – AUSDRUCK FÜR DEN INHALT EINER FLÄCHE [BESTIMMTES I] – UND DER UMKEHRUNG DER DIFFERENTIALRECHNUNG II! DIE INTEGRALRECHNUNG [UNBESTIMMTES I]." INTEGRAL PERSPECTIVE IS NONIDEAL, MULTIDIMENSIONAL, HOLISTIC, AND EVOLUTIONARY." ***

cdc

BROCHURE

Design
Isabel Naegele
Frankfurt, Germany

Art Direction
Isabel Naegele

Creative Direction
Guenther Misof

Production
Marika Kreft

Agency
CDC Communications &
Design Consultancy GmbH

Principal Type
Orator and Letter Gothic

Dimensions
7¾ x 10 in. (19.5 x 25.4 cm)

Ralt/Teil

3.

manufacturing

Annual Report   1997

ESTERLINE TECHNOLOGIES

ANNUAL REPORT

Design
Kerry Leimer and
Marianne Li
Seattle, Washington

Art Direction
Kerry Leimer

Creative Direction
Kerry Leimer

Design Office
Leimer Cross Design

Client
Esterline Technologies, Inc.

Principal Type
Garamond No. 3

Dimensions
8½ x 11 in. (21.6 x 27.9 cm)

Design
Tom Riddle
Minneapolis, Minnesota
. . . .

Art Direction
Tom Riddle
. . . .

Creative Direction
Joe Duffy and David Lubars
. . . .

Programming
Mark Sandau and Leslie
Fandrich
. . . .

Studio
Duffy Design and Interactive
. . . .

Client
Fallon McElligott and Duffy
Design and Interactive
. . . .

Principal Type
Ataribaby and Trade Gothic

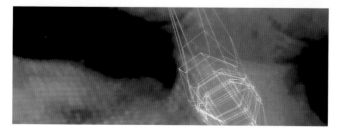

STUDENT WORK
. . . .

Design
Todd Hulin
New York, New York
. . . .

School
New York University
. . . .

Instructor
Craig Kanarick
. . . .

Principal Type
Charlemagne

WHICH IS TO BE SUNG

A HYMN TO RA

ON THE DAY OF THE NEW

E BOAT

HOMAGE TO THEE

THOU ROLLEST ON, LIGHT
THOU SENDEST FORTH

FOR MILLIONS OE YEARS

THOU DECREEST REJOICING FOR EVERY MA

WILL MOST CERTAINLY CAUSE THE ENEM

O HAVE HIS BEING WITH RA, AN

EFNUT, KEB, NUT, OSIRIS, ISIS, [SUT

OASTED. IT IS AN ACT OF PRAISE TO RA AS I

NEW TABLET, WHICH

RAVELLING SHALL BE R

STUDENT WORK

· · · · · · · · · · · · · ·

Design
Todd Hulin
New York, New York

· · · · · · · · · · · · · ·

School
New York University

· · · · · · · · · · · · · ·

Instructor
Mara Kurtz

· · · · · · · · · · · · · ·

Principal Type
Trajan

Ethan HAWKE

He left the big screen for
two years to pen his first novel.
Now the actor starts a
new chapter of his life with
'Great Expectations'

by DAVID LIPSKY

portfolio by MARK SELIGER

TV OPENING

. . . .

Design
Julie Hirschfeld
New York, New York
. . . .

Art Direction
Dede Sullivan
. . . .

Creative Direction
Mike Benson
. . . .

Studio
VH1
. . . .

Principal Type
John Dvl and Synchro

MAGAZINE SPREAD
. . . .
Design
Rina Migliaccio
New York, New York
. . . .
Art Direction
Richard Baker
. . . .
Photo Editor
Jennifer Crandall
. . . .
Studio
US
. . . .
Principal Type
CG Gothic
. . . .
Dimensions
8½ x 20 in. (21.6 x 50.8 cm)

MAGAZINE SPREAD
. . . .
Design
Fred Woodward and Gail
Anderson
New York, New York
. . . .
Art Direction
Fred Woodward
. . . .
Photography
Peggy Sirota
. . . .
Photo Editor
Rachel Knepfer
. . . .
Client
Rolling Stone
. . . .
Principal Type
Champion
. . . .
Dimensions
12 x 20 in. (30.5 x 50.8 cm)

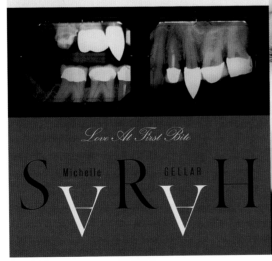

MAGAZINE SPREAD
. . . .
Design
Fred Woodward and Gail
Anderson
New York, New York
. . . .
Art Direction
Fred Woodward
. . . .
Photography
Mark Seliger
. . . .
Photo Editor
Rachel Knepfer
. . . .
Client
Rolling Stone
. . . .
Principal Type
Throhand
. . . .
Dimensions
12 x 20 in. (30.5 x 50.8 cm)

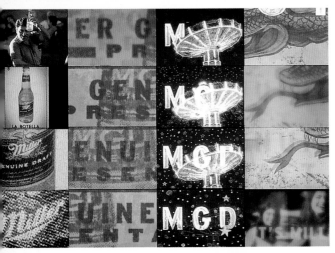

ELECTRONIC MEDIA

. . . .

Design
Hal Wolverton, Heath Lowe,
Matt Eller, Joe Peila, Neil
Gust, and Topher Sinkinson
Portland, Oregon

. . . .

Lettering
Hal Wolverton, Heath Lowe,
Joe Peila, Matt Eller, Sarah
Starr, Alan Foster, Neil Gust,
Mary Kysar, and Topher
Sinkinson

. . . .

Art Direction
Alicia Johnson, Hal
Wolverton, and Heath Lowe

. . . .

Creative Direction
Alicia Johnson and Hal
Wolverton

. . . .

Photography
Melody McDaniel
Los Angeles, California

. . . .

Illustration
Rob and Christian Clayton
Los Angeles, California

. . . .

Agency
Wieden & Kennedy

. . . .

Studio
Johnson & Wolverton

. . . .

Client
Miller Brewing Co.

. . . .

Principal Type
Interstate (modified) and
Champion (modified)

FILM TITLES

. . . .

Design
Michael Riley, Kyle Cooper,
and Eric Smith
Los Angeles, California

. . . .

Direction
Kyle Cooper

. . . .

Producer
Tim Thompson

. . . .

Executive Producer
Chip Houghton

. . . .

Studio
Imaginary Forces

. . . .

Client
Sony Pictures

. . . .

Principal Type
Trajan (modified) and Mason
(modified)

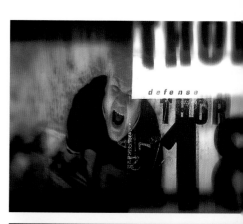

MMERCIAL

· · · · · · · · ·

Feldman
Monica, California

· · · · · · · · ·

ve Direction
stein and Jerry

· · · · · · · · ·

Effects Post
isor
Conroy

· · · · · · · · ·

ive Producer
yers

· · · · · · · · ·

nimation
Caulonga, Robin
Deb Catalano, and
Emerick

· · · · · · · · ·

er
arquis

· · · · · · · · ·

Effects
rendiville

· · · · · · · · ·

Ring of Fire

· · · · · · · · ·

al Type
Bold

TV COMMERCIAL

· · · · · · · · · · · · ·

Design
Christopher Wargin, Ben Go,
and Chris Do
Santa Monica, California

· · · · · · · · · · · · ·

Creative Direction
Christopher Wargin

· · · · · · · · · · · · ·

Studio
PRoGRESS (bureau of
design)

· · · · · · · · · · · · ·

Client
Flying Tiger Films

· · · · · · · · · · · · ·

Principal Type
Gothic 821 Condensed,
Aurora Bold Condensed, and
Eurostile Bold Oblique

MOTION GRAPHICS
. . . .
Design
Jessie Li-Chun Huang
Venice, California
. . . .
Art Direction
Jessie Li-Chun Huang
. . . .
Creative Direction
Christopher Do
. . . .
Agency
Rubin/Postaer & Associates
. . . .
Studio
Blind Visual
Propaganda, Inc.
. . . .
Client
Partnership for a Drug Free
America
. . . .
Principal Type
ITC Franklin Gothic and
handlettering

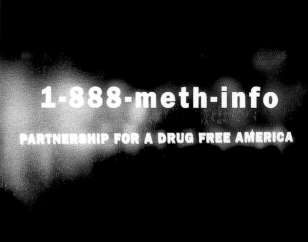

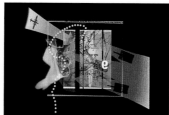

INVITATION

Design
Dave Kotlan
Milwaukee, Wisconsin

Creative Direction
Marc Tebon

Copywriter
Mike Spanjar

Studio
Graphic Solutions, Inc.

Principal Type
Rockwell and Rockwell
Condensed

Dimensions
11 x 34 in. (27.9 x 86.4 cm)

TV OPENING

Design
Elizabeth Rovnick
Santa Monica, California

Art Direction
Elizabeth Rovnick

Animation
Brumby Boylston

Producer
Casey Steele

Executive Producer
Matt Marquis

Studio
Fuel

Client
Slamdance Film Festival

Principal Type
Helvetica, Codesteady, Bell
MT, and News Gothic

Design
John Bielenberg and Chuck
Denison
San Francisco, California

Creative Direction
John Bielenberg

Writer
Chris Williams
Boston, Massachusetts

Design Office
Bielenberg Design

Client
Virtual Telemetrix, Inc.

Principal Type
Helvetica Inserat

Design
Rodrigo Sánchez
Madrid, Spain

Art Direction
Rodrigo Sánchez

Creative Direction
Carmelo Caderot

Studio
Unidad Editorial, S.A.

Client
El Mundo

Principal Type
Giza Seven Nine, Gill Sans,
and Cloister

Dimensions
7⅝ x 11¼ in. (20 x 28.5 cm)

METROPOLI

LA REVISTA DE MADRID. N 423. DEL 3 AL 9 DE JULIO DE 199

RESTAURANTES CON TERRAZA 1998

FORTUNE NO. 197

IF THERE'S A SECRET TO GETTING A JOB IN AN AGENCY'S CREATIVE DEPARTMENT, TAKING THE ADVERTISING PORTFOLIO WORKSHOP IS THE CLOSEST THING TO IT.

LUCKY NUMBERS: 6, 15, 35, 93, 132, 155

FORTUNE NO. 056

GAIN THE KNOWLEDGE TO GROW CREATIVELY.

LUCKY NUMBERS: 5, 10, 22, 67, 98, 115

FORTUNE NO. 516

YOU'LL LEAVE THE WORKSHOP WITH A FINISHED PORTFOLIO THAT SENDS OUT ONE MESSAGE LOUD AND CLEAR: I AM NOT JUST ANOTHER BEGINNER.

LUCKY NUMBERS: 8, 11, 26, 43, 61, 63

FORTUNE NO. 621

THE ADVERTISING PORTFOLIO WORKSHOP SUCCEEDS BECAUSE IT TEACHES THE DISCIPLINES THAT DIVIDE THE AMATEURS FROM THE PROFESSIONALS WITHOUT WASTING TIME ON EASY TECHNIQUES ANYBODY CAN PICK UP.

LUCKY NUMBERS: 2, 5, 98, 133, 340, 445

FORTUNE NO. 208

ALUMNI COME AWAY KNOWING WHAT TO DO WITH JOBS ONCE THEY HAVE THEM.

LUCKY NUMBERS: 1, 25, 33, 84, 110, 208

FORTUNE NO. 440

MORE THAN 100 COPYWRITERS AND ART DIRECTORS OWE THEIR FIRST JOBS TO THE AL HAYES ADVERTISING PORTFOLIO WORKSHOP.

LUCKY NUMBERS: 5, 17, 44, 92, 196, 214

FORTUNE NO. 390

YOUR FUTURE WILL BE TOLD IN TIME.

LUCKY NUMBERS: 19, 21, 85, 77, 91, 121

FORTUNE NO. 616

DURING THE 15-WEEK SESSION, YOU'LL SOLVE 10 VARIED ADVERTISING PROBLEMS UNDER THE SAME KIND OF PRESSURES THAT EXIST IN AGENCIES.

LUCKY NUMBERS: 11, 17, 25, 66, 203, 212

FORTUNE NO. 032

WELL-SOLVED PROBLEMS TURN INTO PORTFOLIO PIECES, PRESENTED ON THE LAST NIGHT AS BEAUTIFUL AND brilliant ADS.

LUCKY NUMBERS: 20, 32, 58, 134, 159, 172

FORTUNE NO. 044

AN IMPORTANT OPPORTUNITY HAS BEEN OFFERED TO YOU. DO NOT MAKE THE MISTAKE MADE BY OTHERS, WHO HAVE DISREGARDED SIMILAR OFFERS IN THE PAST AND NOW LANGUISH IN OBSCURITY.

LUCKY NUMBERS: 8, 23, 50, 77, 92, 440

FORTUNE NO. 069

AGENCIES VIEW WORKSHOP ALUMNI AS WORTH TAKING A CHANCE ON BECAUSE SO MANY HAVE BECOME ADVERTISING STARS.

LUCKY NUMBERS: 11, 19, 24, 31, 39, 50

FORTUNE NO. 225

AL HAYES, CHAIRMAN OF HAYES ORLIE CUNDALL INC., IS A LONG TIME SAN FRANCISCO CREATIVE DIRECTOR AND WINNER OF MORE LOCAL, REGIONAL AND NATIONAL AWARDS THAN HE CAN REMEMBER. CURRENTLY, AL IS FOCUSING ON WHAT HE CALLS "THE REAL BUSINESS OF ADVERTISING: MAKING ADS THAT BUILD AN AGENCY BECAUSE THEY BUILD THE CLIENTS THE AGENCY SERVES." HAYES ORLIE CUNDALL HAS HELPED BUILD CLIENTS LIKE KAISER PERMANENTE, CHEVRON CHEMICAL, ROUND TABLE PIZZA, BIRKENSTOCK, KONICA AND DELTA DENTAL.

LUCKY NUMBERS: 16, 18, 30, 32, 46, 92

FORTUNE NO. 623

KNOWLEDGE IS POWER.

LUCKY NUMBERS: 7, 21, 45, 101, 223, 250

FORTUNE NO. 764

YOU WILL DEVELOP THE PORTFOLIO YOU NEED TO SECURE A JOB AS AN ENTRY-LEVEL COPYWRITER OR ART DIRECTOR IN THE CREATIVE DEPARTMENT OF A GOOD ADVERTISING AGENCY.

LUCKY NUMBERS: 3, 8, 64, 73, 107, 420

FORTUNE NO. 426

WORKSHOPS ARE HELD IN BOTH THE FALL AND THE SPRING AND MAY BE REPEATED TO IMPROVE YOUR PORTFOLIO.

LUCKY NUMBERS: 2, 18, 23, 41, 59, 66

FORTUNE NO. 863

DROP ANOTHER COIN IN SLOT AND I WILL TELL YOU MORE.

LUCKY NUMBERS: 12, 51, 70, 86, 92, 100

FORTUNE NO. 582

THE ADVERTISING PORTFOLIO WORKSHOP, TAUGHT BY AL HAYES, BEGAN IN 1974 AND HAS GARNERED PRAISE AND ATTENTION FROM THE ADVERTISING INDUSTRY EVER SINCE.

LUCKY NUMBERS: 17, 36, 50, 76, 88, 90

FORTUNE NO. 329

THE AMERICAN ADVERTISING FEDERATION NOMINATED AL HAYES FOR ITS 1991 DISTINGUISHED ADVERTISING EDUCATOR AWARD, GIVEN EACH YEAR TO AMERICA'S MOST EFFECTIVE ADVERTISING TEACHER.

LUCKY NUMBERS: 13, 21, 32, 58, 62, 54

FORTUNE NO. 567

MEET CREATIVE CHALLENGES AND LEARN IMPORTANT INSIGHTS! DAZZLE YOUR COLLEAGUES AND BOOST YOUR CAREER—SIGN UP TODAY!

LUCKY NUMBERS: 19, 20, 27, 32, 33, 50

SAN FRANCISCO AGENCIES ARE LOUSY WITH AL HAYES ALUMNI. HE'S AS CLOSE TO A GODFATHER AS THE BUSINESS HAS. THE AL HAYES COURSE IS A RITE OF PASSAGE, A TRIAL BY FIRE. I'LL TELL YOU A SECRET: MOST OF THE WRITERS AND ART DIRECTORS IN TOWN HAVE AL TATTOOED ON THEIR FOREARMS. I KNOW I DO.

—MICHAEL PATRICK COLLINS CREATIVE DIRECTOR ABINGTON BERTRAM NOBLE ADVERTISING

ARTISTS IN PRINT
665 THIRD ST. SUITE 530
SAN FRANCISCO CA 94107

AUTO

---

you don't happen to have a great portfolio, you can... her work at a relatively bad... way for years & get a piece of good work. Very now & then you can take Al's class... out half of the really good student portfolios that come... Al's class come out of the... his class.

Jeff Goodby
Creative Director / Principal
Goodby Berlin & Silverstein

ARTISTS IN PRINT
665 Third St.
Suite 530
San Francisco, CA
94107

32

FORTUNE NO. 006

A WISE MAN, RESPECTED AND HONORED, WILL PRESENT YOU WITH CHALLENGES AND IMPORTANT INSIGHTS. YOU WILL WORK HARD AND DEVELOP YOUR INNER STRENGTH.

LUCKY NUMBERS: 42, 57, 60, 86, 122, 301

FORTUNE NO. 402

EACH WORKSHOP IS COMPRISED OF 15 SESSIONS WHICH MEET ON Wednesday NIGHTS FROM 6:30 TO 9:30PM AT FORT MASON CENTER.

LUCKY NUMBERS: 3, 8, 24, 32, 39, 58

FORTUNE NO. 376

THE ADVERTISING PORTFOLIO WORKSHOP IS LIMITED TO 25 STUDENTS PER 15-WEEK SESSION.

LUCKY NUMBERS: 4, 5, 10, 16, 24, 40

FORTUNE NO. 186

AMAZING! ARTISTS IN PRINT OFFERS YOU A RARE OPPORTUNITY TO EXPAND YOUR KNOWLEDGE AND INFLUENCE YOUR FUTURE.

LUCKY NUMBERS: 2, 8, 14, 23, 29, 52

FORTUNE NO. 016

MAIL REGISTRATION AND/OR MEMBERSHIP APPLICATION TO: ARTISTS IN PRINT 665 THIRD STREET, SUITE 530, SAN FRANCISCO, CA 94107 OR FAX TO 415 362 1989 PHOTOCOPIES OF THIS REGISTRATION ARE ACCEPTABLE.

FORTUNE NO. 354

NAME
TITLE
COMPANY
MAILING ADDRESS
CITY / STATE / ZIP
PHONE   FAX

FORTUNE NO. 115

THE NEXT WORKSHOP SESSION BEGINS:

AL HAYES PORTFOLIO WORKSHOP
FALL/OCTOBER 7

FORTUNE NO. 248

TUITION   ☐ $350 PER PERSON WITH CURRENT AIP MEMBERSHIP
              OR BY JOINING AT THE TIME OF REGISTRATION
           ☐ $400 PER PERSON FOR NON-MEMBERS
MEMBERSHIP ☐ $45 INDIVIDUAL
           ☐ $25 STUDENT
              STUDENT MEMBERS MUST ATTEND CLASSES A MINIMUM OF
              12 HOURS PER WEEK AND ARE REQUIRED TO VOLUNTEER 12
              HOURS TO AIP DURING THE FIRST 90 DAYS OF THEIR MEM-
              BERSHIP. PLEASE ENCLOSE A COPY OF YOUR CURRENT I.D.
           ☐ $85 BUSINESS
              BUSINESS MEMBERSHIPS BENEFIT UP TO FIVE EMPLOYEES.
              PLEASE COMPLETE ONE APPLICATION PER EMPLOYEE.

FORTUNE NO. 153

TOTAL PAYMENT
FORM OF PAYMENT ☐ CHECK ENCLOSED (PAYABLE TO ARTISTS IN PRINT)
                ☐ MASTERCARD / VISA
                ACCOUNT NO.
SIGNATURE   EXPIRES

---

aip

ANNUAL REPORT

Design
Kevin Roberson
San Francisco, California

Art Direction
Bill Cahan

Creative Direction
Bill Cahan

Agency
Cahan & Associates

Client
Vivus, Inc.

Principal Type
Futura

Dimensions
9¼ x 11¾ in. (23.5 x 29.9 cm)

▶

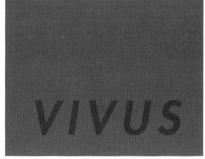

In 1997, VIVUS established MUSE® (alprostadil) in the United States as a first line therapy for treatment of erectile dysfunction: MUSE was launched in January of 1997 and by the end of the year, more than 825,000 prescriptions were written and 8 million units sold, thus establishing MUSE in the United States as a leading treatment for erectile dysfunction by urologists and as one of the top 35 most successful first year pharmaceutical products ever.

Local problem, local solution. Experts agree that for many men erectile dysfunction is a local disorder; consequently, the transurethral delivery of treatment provided by MUSE is a novel, local solution to this local problem. MUSE provides the patient, partner and physician a convenient and minimally invasive treatment which explains, in large part, its rapid acceptance and use in 1997.

Alprostadil safety and efficacy. First licensed as a pharmaceutical in 1981, the safety and efficacy of alprostadil as a therapeutic agent is well established. Experimental intracavernosal injection of alprostadil for the treatment of erectile dysfunction began in the late 1980s and culminated with Food and Drug Administration (FDA) clearance of alprostadil for injection therapy of erectile dysfunction in 1995. VIVUS began clinical trials in 1992, and in five short years, successfully demonstrated that alprostadil also can be delivered safely and effectively via the urethra using a small, plastic applicator rather than a needle.

Novel drug delivery. MUSE uses a novel drug delivery system which consists of a single-use, prefilled plastic applicator designed for easy handling, administration and disposal. The small size of the applicator provides both patient and partner with a discreet and easy-to-use treatment option.

POSTER

Design
Mimi O'Chun and Victoria Pohlmann
San Francisco, California

Lettering
Mimi O'Chun

Art Direction
David Salanitro

Creative Direction
David Salanitro

Photography
Dave Magnusson, Mimi O'Chun, and Hunter Wimmer

Agency
Oh Boy, A Design Company

Client
Artists in Print's Al Hayes Workshop

Principal Type
Trade Gothic

Dimensions
24 x 36 in. (61 x 91.4 cm)

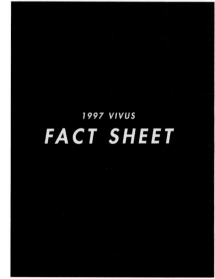

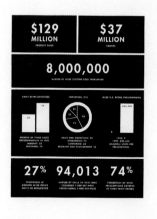

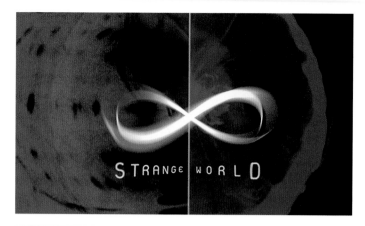

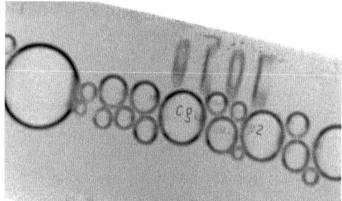

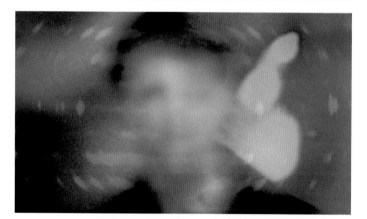

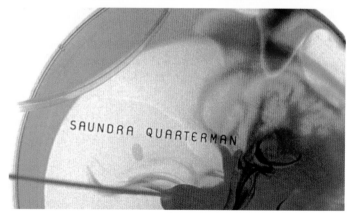

TV OPENING

. . . .

Design
Olivia D'Albis, Dana Yee,
and Karin Fong
Los Angeles, California

. . . .

Art Direction
Karin Fong

. . . .

Creative Direction
Peter Frankfurt

. . . .

Producer
Candy Renick

. . . .

Editor
Mark Hoffman

. . . .

Animation
Matt Cullen and Martin
Von Will

. . . .

Studio
Imaginary Forces

. . . .

Client
Teakwood Lane Production
and Fox Studios

. . . .

Principal Type
Platelet

STATIONERY

Design
Stefan G. Bucher
Pasadena, California

Art Direction
Stefan G. Bucher

Studio
344 Design, LLC

Principal Type
Helvetica

Dimensions
17¼ x 14⅛ in. (43.8 x 35.9 cm)

three forty four design

101 n. grand avenue, suite 7   pasadena, ca 91103
tel/fax: 626.796.5148   e-mail: three44@earthlink.net

three forty four design
Stefan G. Bucher

101 n. grand avenue, suite 7   pasadena, ca 91103
tel/fax: 626.796.5148   e-mail: three44@earthlink.net

POSTER
. . . .

Design
Heath Lowe, Hal Wolverton,
and Mary Kysar
Portland, Oregon
. . . .

Lettering
Hal Wolverton, Heath Lowe,
Joe Peila, Sarah Starr, Alan
Foster, Neil Gust, Mary
Kysar, and Topher Sinkinson
. . . .

Art Direction
Alicia Johnson and Hal
Wolverton
. . . .

Creative Direction
Alicia Johnson and Hal
Wolverton
. . . .

Agency
Wieden & Kennedy
. . . .

Studio
Johnson & Wolverton
. . . .

Client
Miller Brewing Co.
. . . .

Principal Type
Interstate
. . . .

Dimensions
120 x 36 in. (304.8 x
91.4 cm)

ELECTRONIC
LOGOTYPE
. . . .

Design
Hal Wolverton, Heath Lowe,
Joe Peila, Alan Foster, Mary
Kysar, Sarah Starr, Neil Gust,
and Topher Sinkinson
Portland, Oregon
. . . .

Lettering
Hal Wolverton, Heath Lowe,
Joe Peila, Matt Eller, Sarah
Starr, Alan Foster, Neil Gust,
Mary Kysar, and Topher
Sinkinson
. . . .

Art Direction
Alicia Johnson and Hal
Wolverton
. . . .

Creative Direction
Alicia Johnson and Hal
Wolverton
. . . .

Photography
Melody McDaniel
Los Angeles, California
. . . .

Illustration
Rob and Christian Clayton
Los Angeles, California
. . . .

Agency
Wieden & Kennedy
. . . .

Studio
Johnson & Wolverton
. . . .

Client
Miller Brewing Co.
. . . .

Principal Type
Interstate (modified)

OPENING ANIMATION
. . . .

Design
Jakob Trollbeck
New York, New York
. . . .

Creative Direction
Jakob Trollbeck
. . . .

Animators
Arman Matin and Jakob
Trollbeck
. . . .

Studio
R/Greenberg Associates
. . . .

Client
The TED Conferences
. . . .

Principal Type
Helvetica Neue Black

OPENING ANIMATION
. . . .

Design
Jakob Trollbeck
New York, New York
. . . .

Creative Direction
Jakob Trollbeck
. . . .

Animator
Jakob Trollbeck
. . . .

Studio
R/Greenberg Associates
. . . .

Client
The TED Conferences
. . . .

Principal Type
Folio Bold Condensed

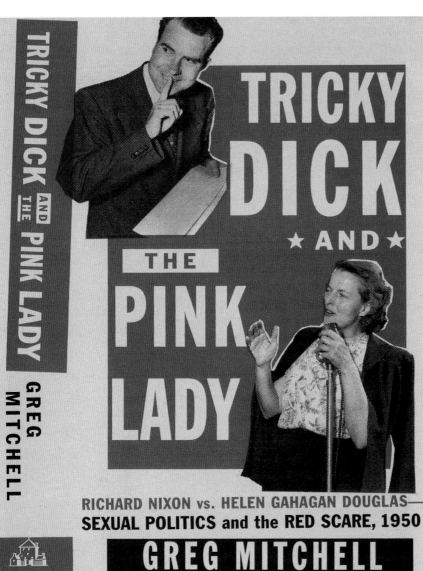

BOOK COVER

. . . .

Design
Gabrielle Bordwin
New York, New York

. . . .

Art Direction
Robbin Schiff

. . . .

Photography
UPI/Corbis-Bettmann

. . . .

Studio
Random House, Inc.

. . . .

Principal Type
Franklin Gothic Extra
Condensed

. . . .

Dimensions
7⅜ x 9½ in. (18.6 x 24.1 cm)

PACKAGING

. . . .

Design
Chad Hagen
Minneapolis, Minnesota

. . . .

Lettering
Chad Hagen

. . . .

Creative Direction
Bill Thorburn

. . . .

Copywriter
Kathi Skow

. . . .

Agency
Carmichael Lynch Thorburn

. . . .

Client
Carmichael Lynch

. . . .

Principal Type
Bitstream Schadow, Adobe
American Typewriter, Adobe
Cooper Black, and Adobe
Helvetica

. . . .

Dimensions
5 x 13 in. (12.7 x 33 cm)

WORDS OF WISDOM.

JAMES MONTALBANO Being co-chairman two years in a row gives you an opportunity to do some things differently and, hopefully, a little better the second time around. This year, we did away with the submission templates that caused so much distress last year. And, while it was refreshing to see typographic samples in a variety of styles, it was disappointing to see that some people chose to present their work in a very meager way, giving the judges little to look at. In a certain respect, this concentrated the judging experience, allowing the judges to quickly move through those submissions and concentrate on the well-presented work. Since it was the responsibility of the judges to look at typefaces working as typefaces, and not just a collection of letterforms, those entries that showed the typeface working in its appropriate environment received the most scrutiny and discussion. The most interesting thing for me was to see each judge's unique style and point of view emerge from these discussions. While it would be an interesting record of the competition to somehow record these discussions, I don't know if everyone would be delighted with what was said about every submission. Perhaps it's best to let the judges just pick the winners. I would like to thank the judges for their energy and perseverance, and I would like to thank everyone who entered, and invite you all to do it again next year.

TDC²

PAUL SHAW The second TDC² competition confirmed the diversity of the current typographic scene. The select number of winners—approximately ten percent of the total number of entries—reflected the mixed backgrounds and high standards of the judges and underscored how much type design has changed in the last fifteen years. The judges looked beyond the surface beauty of the individual characters to check how well drawn they were and how they performed as type. The judges were a tough audience and the discussions among them pointed to how much disagreement there is, even within the top ranks of the profession, over the criteria for a good typeface. For James Montalbano and me these discussions were very illuminating and proved to be the highlight of the judging process. It is a shame that they were not recorded for inclusion in the annual.

On a personal note, my favorite typeface in the show is the complex and stunning Zapfino. While everyone was excited by Hermann Zapf's latest design, there seemed to be an undercurrent of puzzlement over its usefulness. My response is: damn functionality and just enjoy beauty when it appears.

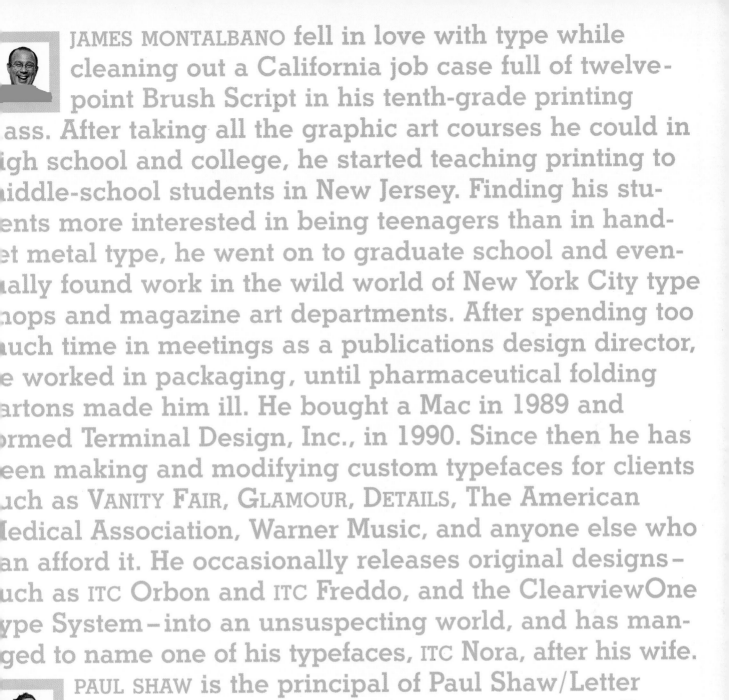

JAMES MONTALBANO fell in love with type while cleaning out a California job case full of twelve-point Brush Script in his tenth-grade printing class. After taking all the graphic art courses he could in high school and college, he started teaching printing to middle-school students in New Jersey. Finding his students more interested in being teenagers than in hand-set metal type, he went on to graduate school and eventually found work in the wild world of New York City type shops and magazine art departments. After spending too much time in meetings as a publications design director, he worked in packaging, until pharmaceutical folding cartons made him ill. He bought a Mac in 1989 and formed Terminal Design, Inc., in 1990. Since then he has been making and modifying custom typefaces for clients such as VANITY FAIR, GLAMOUR, DETAILS, The American Medical Association, Warner Music, and anyone else who can afford it. He occasionally releases original designs—such as ITC Orbon and ITC Freddo, and the ClearviewOne Type System—into an unsuspecting world, and has managed to name one of his typefaces, ITC Nora, after his wife.

PAUL SHAW is the principal of Paul Shaw/Letter Design, a small studio that specializes in calligraphy, typography, and type design. Among his clients are Campbell Soup, Rolex, Clairol, VANITY FAIR, GRP Records, Parham Santana, Crowley Webb and Associates, Studio Robilant, Apple Designsource, and Indika NY. He is also a partner with Garrett Boge in the digital-type foundry LetterPerfect. He and Boge recently designed The Swedish Set, a group of three fonts (Stockholm, Göteborg, and Uppsala) for Agfa. For the past thirteen years Paul has taught calligraphy and typography at Parsons School of Design.

Judges

BARBARA GLAUBER

Barbara Glauber received a BFA from SUNY/Purchase and an MFA from California Institute of the Arts. In her New York–based studio, Heavy Meta, Barbara focuses on the design of publications, information graphics, packaging, and other materials for clients in the art and entertainment industries. She curated the 1993 exhibition LIFT AND SEPARATE: GRAPHIC DESIGN AND THE QUOTE UNQUOTE VERNACULAR at the Cooper Union, as well as edited its accompanying publication. She served as the chair for the eighteenth annual American Center for Design 100 SHOW. Barbara teaches graphic design at Yale University and The Cooper Union.

HANS EDUARD MEIER

Hans Eduard Meier apprenticed as a compositor before attending the Zurich Kunstgewerbeschule (School of Arts and Crafts). He then worked in Zurich and Paris as a graphic designer. From 1950 to 1986 he taught typography and drawing at the Zurich Kunstgewerbeschule. DIE SCHRIFTENSENTWICKLUNG (THE DEVELOPMENT OF LETTERFORMS), his trilingual textbook, has gone through eleven editions since its initial publication in 1959. In 1984 Meier began a collaboration with the Institute for Computer Systems in Zurich. He is the designer of Syntax, ITC Syndor, Barbedor, and Lapidar typefaces. A serif version of Syntax is currently in progress.

DENNIS ORTIZ-LOPEZ

Dennis Ortiz-Lopez studied technical rendering at Compton College in Compton, California. Since 1974 his intricate and precise handlettering has graced the pages of ROLLING STONE, SPORTS ILLUSTRATED, and many other American, British, and German magazines. He has designed logotypes, headlines, and fonts for these magazines and since 1993 has sold his fonts under the O-L name through Fonthaus. Dennis is noted for his love of nineteenth-century letters, especially those found in wood type. In the 1980s he taught courses in graphic design methodology and lettering at the School of Visual Arts.

FREDA SACK

Freda Sack studied typographic design at the Maidstone College of Art & School of Printing. She began her type design career in 1972, drawing and stencil cutting headline typefaces in the Letraset studio. She later worked for Fonts and Typographic Systems International. Since 1990 she has been a partner with David Quay in The Foundry. She has lectured in Austria, Germany, Norway, and Pakistan. Her work has been in EYE, GRAPHICS INTERNATIONAL, TYPOGRAPHIC, CIRCULAR, and DESIGN WEEK. Freda is co-chair and a fellow of the international Society of Typographic Designers. She also organizes the group's biennial TypoGraphic Awards.

Brunel Railtrack Signage Font
Kings Cross Paddington Norbiton
Newquay Newlyn Woolwich Perth
Arsenal Norbiton Surbiton East
Cheam Horley Sanderstead Soho
Victoria Clapham Junction Brixton
Greenwich Ladywell Bristol Leeds
Fulwell Strawberry Fields Forever
Penge Lewisham Herne Hill Crewe
Brighton Purley Raynes Park York
Stockwell Earlsfield Cardiff Bath
Edinburgh Cardiff Manchester Hull
Glasgow Central Wigan Aberdeen

Brunel designed by The Foundry designers Freda Sack and
David Quay. Brunel is the new signing typeface which gives
Railtrack a visible presence within the plethora of identities
of private operating companies which now make up the UK
railway system. It identifies the properties owned by the
company — the track and the stations. The typeface has two
versions, Brunel Positive and Brunel Negative which in
reversed out signs appears the same weight, but which is
actually lighter. The Brunel typefaces form a significant part
of Railtrack's new identity. They were commissioned by
design director Paul Mann at Lloyd Northover Citigate.

OLEgyptian Display for the Macintosh

(&.,:;!?""""·$¢£'"#%*/{|}[\])ABCDEFGHIJKLMNOPQRSTU
VWXYZabcdefghijklmnopqrsßtuvwxyz0123456789
(&.,:;!?""""·$¢£'"#%/{|}[\])ABCDEFGHIJKLMNOPQRSTU*
VWXYZabcdefghijklmnopqrsßtuvwxyz0123456789
(&.,:;!?""""·$¢£'"#%*/{|}[\])ABCDEFGHIJKLMNOPQRSTU
VWXYZabcdefghijklmnopqrsßtuvwxyz0123456789
(&.,:;!?""""·$¢£'"#%/{|}[\])ABCDEFGHIJKLMNOPQRSTU*
VWXYZabcdefghijklmnopqrsßtuvwxyz0123456789
(&.,:;!?""""·$¢£'"#%*/{|}[\])ABCDEFGHIJKLMNOPQRSTUV
WXYZabcdefghijklmnopqrsßtuvwxyz0123456789
(&.,:;!?""""·$¢£'"#%*/{|}[\])ABCDEFGHIJKLMNOPQRSTUV
WXYZabcdefghijklmnopqrsßtuvwxyz0123456789
(&.,:;!?""""·$¢£'"#%*/{|}[\])ABCDEFGHIJKLMNOPQRSTUV
WXYZabcdefghijklmnopqrsßtuvwxyz0123456789

OLEgyptian is based upon a classic sans serif form structured with egyptian-styled square serifs. This is one of the few fonts that I have designed for text as well as display, and one of the very few designs with more than one weight. *OLEgyptian* comes in four weights, light, medium and bold with italics and an Extra Bold. The medium also comes with an alternate character set as well as an alternate italic for text sizes.

DENNIS ORTIZ-LOPEZ JUDGE'S WORK

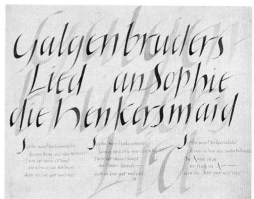

HANS EDUARD MEIER JUDGE'S WORK

BARBARA GLAUBER

Excessively embellished and exuberantly intertwined, Antionette is a nineteen-nineties/nineteenth-century hybrid that I would classify as "Extreme Victorian." Rather than revisiting the elaborate letterforms of the Victorian era, designer Lee Schulz turns instead to Victorian ornament for inspiration. The unconventionally curlicued letterforms reach beyond their allotted character widths and, unlike Victorians, touch their neighbors. It's practically impossible to escape from the incessant decoration—even the space bar is adorned. Blocks of text set in Antionette are challenging to read, but they recall wrought iron gates, creating an impenetrable facade that dares the reader to find the words hidden within. The intricate patterns it creates are beautiful and I love the idea of a pattern-generating system rooted in language – think of the possibilities for incorporating subliminal messages and monograms into ads and annual reports! While Antionette may not be ideal for choking posters and stop signs, I am dying to find a use for this innovative, zesty typeface in my work.

One annoying thing about this typeface: Lee seems to have spelled the name incorrectly (it should be Antoinette not Antionette). I am writing to him to see if he can change it, otherwise it looks kind of stupid.

Antionette stemmed from a larger idea within my graduate thesis project. My intent was to create a mechanism for generating ornamental forms for my design work. The letterforms were derived from an obsessive study of the form-making of the Victorian period, celebrating the abundance and self-indulgence of Victorian ornament. Everything – from the letterforms to the space and option space – is ornamented, and the characters are designed to fit together very particularly so that patterns can be created by simply repeating characters. The purpose was to create an immersing tool that clearly evoked my critique and allows no escape.

TYPEFACE
· · · · · · · · · · · · · ·

Typeface Designer
Lee Schulz
Boston, Massachusetts
· · · · · · · · · · · · · ·

Typeface Name
Antionette

TYPEFACE
. . . .

Typeface Designer
Serge Pichii
North Vancouver, British
Columbia, Canada
. . . .

Typeface Name
SP Cutouts

··

Hans Eduard Meier said of this typeface:

The work submitted by Serge Pichii, which I consider to be the best of show, is artistically superb. The abstractions of the figurative motifs constitute a true unity of design, and they embody a high level of artistry. The pictograms are easily understandable, despite their strongly abstracted type of execution.

Freda Sack said of this typeface:

I was disappointed that out of the 123 typeface entries in this competition there were few fonts that had any originality—so much of the work regurgitated old ideas. Unfortunately the predominant trend is still to take an existing typeface idea and adapt it. Also, some of the work could have been better presented to show the intended use of the typeface.

My Judge's Choice was curiously not a typeface, but a stunning set of symbols in a pi font—a very powerful set of designs that leaped up from the judging table with a visual excitement that most of the typefaces lacked. The graphic symbols, each one a little gem, were simple and effective in their design—strong lines and shapes, contained, but full of energy. They were reminiscent of naive African art. I was immediately aware that whoever designed this pi font had a good understanding of design with a very fine eye for use of space and line. They were completely sure of what they were doing. It was evident that each character had been designed with thought and care. The contrast of negative and positive shape, together with just the right amount of tension of line, produced individual characters that reminded me of well-designed marquees; the simplest and most well thought out ideas are the best—they have a dynamic timelessness.

The idea for the SP Cutouts was inspired by one of my favorite time periods: the early sixties.

The design was influenced by the linocuts and woodcuts that were so in vogue at the time. I wanted to keep that special feeling of high contrast with its vast masses of solid black color and sharp white lines, while making the images compatible with today's digital technology.

Each image can stand alone as a spot illustration. Keying them in without spaces allows for more unified and sophisticated illustrations. The typeface was designed as a set of elements of modules, which can be scaled and combined together in many different ways in order to create more customized illustrations. Special attention has been paid to relationships between elements of every image, so that they withstand downsizing with no loss of details.

DENNIS ORTIZ-LOPEZ

I have always loved classic typefaces. Before the digital revolution, I would draw and redraw the same letters from the same few alphabets over and over in the course of putting together the intricate ornamentations that became my trademark. When I went digital I was faced with a huge problem: my favorite typefaces did not exist in a digital form. Not only did I have to learn how to draw all over again, but I had to do it quickly enough to be able to recreate the typefaces that were the tools of my trade. I took a three-month sabbatical and drew day and night until I managed to finish twenty-four of my most widely used faces from two-inch film fonts and showings that I had archived.

Although I had originally planned these fonts to be my personal tools, they quickly became viable commodities. I had close to ten thousand dollars in sales the first year, followed by a sharp decline in sales the following year. This taught me a lesson: I can't make a living selling fonts alone. And even worse, I realized that if I did intend to sell fonts, I had to go back to designing new ones instead of just resurrecting old ones. Dream on. I had to take what work I could to continue to be competitive and my free time became more and more scarce. Although I have tried, I have yet to achieve the level of proficiency of which I was capable prior to my use of the computer.

There is also the problem of originality. Of those twenty-four fonts that I created, not one was an original design. All became my versions of the original alphabets that they were based upon. How could I take credit for designing something that was designed by someone else and simply recreated by me?

Well, it seems that I could take lessons in plagiarism. This year's contest was plagued by entries that, while claiming originality, were merely recreations of existing typefaces. Some entries were so close to the originals that they were exact copies, still claiming originality. I was appalled. Before judging a piece by its merits, I had to determine if it was an original. I felt more like an art appraiser than a judge, waving my imaginary black light at the submitted samples. All too frequently the imaginary "overpaint" would reveal the framework of an existing typeface, sometimes even a substandard version, complete with the feel of a scanner's touch and enhanced by the infamous auto-trace command.

I chose Akira Kobayashi's ITC Silvermoon for my Judge's Choice because I liked it. Graceful and clean, it had the added distinction of not being familiar to me and, as such, had a flavor of originality. Good inspiration for me to design more fonts.

ITC Silvermoon was inspired by the handwritten headlines in a fashion magazine of the 1930s. I wanted to design a very thin, almost fragile, display type to match illustrations such as those made by Erté. To achieve the elegance of Art Deco style, I made the letterforms very slim, and added a curlicue to some letters. The flow of the curlicue softens the overall look of the typeface. The regular weight is monoline, a single thin stroke, but for the bold I added dramatic shading to create a contrast between thick and thin strokes.

abcdefghijklmnopqrstuvwxyz
ABCDEFGHIJKLMNOPQRSTUVWXYZ
0123456789
ÇÆŒØçøæœfifl[](){}!¡?¿$¢£€#%&@§¶*,.:;""''«»

abcdefghijklmnopqrstuvwxyz
ABCDEFGHIJKLMNOPQRSTUVWXYZ
0123456789
ÇÆŒØçøæœfifl[](){}!¡?¿$¢£€#%&@§¶*,.:;""''«»

TYPEFACE

Typeface Designer
Akira Kobayashi
Tokyo, Japan

Foundry
International Typeface
Corporation

Client
International Typeface
Corporation

Typeface Name
ITC Silvermoon

**Members of Typeface
Family/System**
ITC Silvermoon Regular and
ITC Silvermoon Bold

Entries

Selected

for

Typographic

Excellence

TYPEFACE

· · · · · · · · · · · · ·

Typeface Designer
Akira Kobayashi
Tokyo, Japan

· · · · · · · · · · · · ·

Foundry
International Typeface
Corporation

· · · · · · · · · · · · ·

Client
International Typeface
Corporation

· · · · · · · · · · · · ·

Typeface Name
ITC Japanese Garden

· · · · · · · · · · · · ·

**Members of Typeface
Family/System**
Ornaments

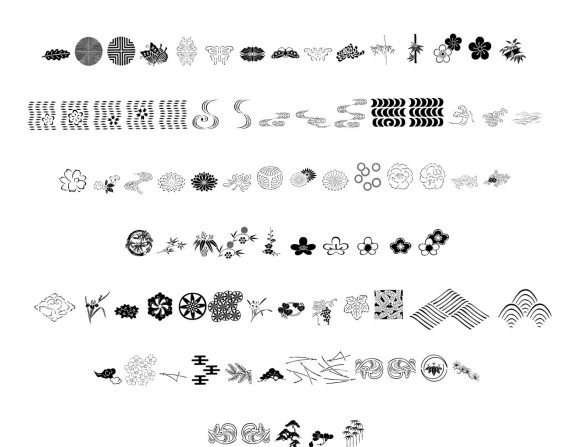

TYPEFACE

· · · · · · · · · · · ·

Typeface Designer
Baruch Gorkin
New York, New York

· · · · · · · · · · · ·

Foundry
Monotype

· · · · · · · · · · · ·

Client
Apple and Microsoft

· · · · · · · · · · · ·

Typeface Name
Arial Hebrew

· · · · · · · · · · · ·

**Members of Typeface
Family/System**
Arial Hebrew Regular and
Arial Hebrew Bold

אבגדהוזח abcdefgh

טיכךלמםנןסע ijklmnopqrstu

פףצץקרשת vwxyz

ויהי בימי אחשורוש (הוא אחשורוש המלך
מהדו ועד כוש שבע ועשרים ומאה מדינה
בימים ההם כשבת המלך אחשורוש על
כסא מלכותו אשר בשושן הבירה בשנת שלש
למלכו עשה משתה לכל שריו ועבדיו
חיל פרס ומדי הפרתמים ושרי המדינות לפניו.

And it came to pass in the days of
Ahasuerus—the Ahasuerus who reigned
from Hodu to Cush over a hundred and
twenty seven provinces—that in those days,
when king Ahasuerus sat on his royal throne
which was in Shushan the capitol, in the
third year of his reign, he made a feast for all
his officials and his servants the army
of Persia and Media, the nobles and the
officilas of the countries before him.

airport

שדה תעופה

Laika was put into space to study
the effects of weightlessness on type.

Look at this paragraph upside down
and note how the top parts of letters
are heavier than the bottom ones.

aabcdefgghijkllmnopqrstuvwxyz*aabcdefgghijklmno
pqrstuvwxyz***aabcdefgghijkllmnopqrstuvwxyz**ABC
DEFGHIJKLMNOPQRSTUVWXYZ*ABCDEFGHIJKLMNO
PQRSTUVWXYZ***ABCDEFGHIJKLMNOPQRSTUVWXYZ**

0123456789:;!?{&&fffifïffiffiß}+×¼½¾→←↓↑(»åçéîñøüæœÅÇÉÎÑØÆŒ«)[@©®™$¢£¥§¶#%*ªº]

The Laika type follows the top-heavy proportion and the emphasis of the horizontal as developed by Roger Excoffon for his *Antique Olive* design (1962) and later employed by Evert Bloemsma in *Balance* (1993). The strategy to make the top parts of letters bigger and heavier than the bottom part **(a reversion of the orthodox sense of harmony in art history)** is based on Emile Javal's 1887 study »Hygiène de la Lecture« which showed that the legibility of type-faces is rooted in the top part of letters. **The Laika family has been used as the main text type in the 1999–2002 California Institute of the Arts catalog, designed by Michael Worthington and Geoff McFetridge.**

TYPEFACE

· · · · · · · · · · · ·

Typeface Designer
Jens Gehlhaar
Los Angeles, California

· · · · · · · · · · · ·

Client
California Institute of the
Arts

Typeface Name
Laika

· · · · · · · · · · · ·

**Members of Typeface
Family/System**
Laika Light Roman, Laika
Light Italic, and Laika Bold
Roman

TYPEFACE

· · · · · · · · · · · · · · · ·

Typeface Designer
Eric Fowles
Louisville, Colorado

· · · · · · · · · · · · · · · ·

Typeface Name
Risso Light

RISSO

HOMEGROWN OUT WEST

QUALITY

1895

FOR DISPLAY ONLY

ABCDEFGHIJKLMNOPQRSTUVWXYZ
1234567890 &.,;?!⋆ AE ST RS ∞ W

TYPEFACE

· · · · · · · · · · · · · ·

Typeface Designer
Professor Hermann Zapf
Darmstadt, Germany

· · · · · · · · · · · · · ·

Foundry
Linotype Library

· · · · · · · · · · · · · ·

Typeface Name
Zapfino

· · · · · · · · · · · · · ·

**Members of Typeface
Family/System**
Zapfino One, Zapfino Two,
Zapfino Three, Zapfino Four,
Zapfino Ligatures, and
Zapfino Ornaments

*A new Script Typeface
from
Linotype Library GmbH
by
Hermann Zapf*

Armenian
Alphabet

Մենք քիչ ենք սակայն մեկ հայ են ասում:
Մենք մեկ ոչ ոքից չենք գերադասում:
Պարկապես մենք էլ պիտի ընդունենք,
Որ մենք միայն մենք Արարատ ունենք...

Պ.ՍԵՎԱԿ

Նախ կապույտ է, կապույտ, կապույտ ...
Հետո Ճերմակ, Ճերմակ, Ճերմակ ...
Հետո երկու հսկա զմբեք
Կապույտների սիրտը հասած,
Նախաստեղծման ծուխերի մեջ
Աստվածների վեձր լսած,
Նոյ նախահոր փարքը տեսած
ՈՒ խոյացած որպես հսկա
Վկայություն, լռած հավետ:

Մարո Մարգարյան

TYPEFACE

. . . .

Typeface Designer
Manvel Shmavonyan
Moscow, Russia

Foundry
ParaType Ltd.

Typeface Name
Asmik

Script
Armenian

**Members of Typeface
Family/System**
Asmik Book, Asmik Italic,
Asmik Bold, and Asmik Bold
Italic

Տառատեսակը
ստեղծվել է
1998 թ.

►

TYPEFACE

. . . .

Typeface Designer
Luc(as) de Groot
Berlin, Germany

Foundry
TheTypes.com

Typeface Name
TheAntiquaB

**Members of Typeface
Family/System**
TheAntiquaB Light,
TheAntiquaB Light Italic,
TheAntiquaB Light Caps,
TheAntiquaB Semi Light,
TheAntiquaB Semi Light
Italic, TheAntiquaB Semi
Light Caps, TheAntiquaB
Regular, TheAntiquaB Italic,
TheAntiquaB Caps,
TheAntiquaB Semi Bold,
TheAntiquaB Semi Bold
Italic, TheAntiquaB Semi
Bold Caps, TheAntiquaB
Bold, TheAntiquaB Bold
Italic, TheAntiquaB Bold
Caps, TheAntiquaB Extra
Bold, TheAntiquaB Extra
Bold Italic, TheAntiquaB
Extra Bold Caps,
TheAntiquaB Black,
TheAntiquaB Black Italic,
and TheAntiquaB Black Caps

TheAntiquaB

THEANTIQUAB-LIGHT 7 PT HOW CAN ONE SET A TEXT collection in a slab serif font! Misuse of FFTheSerif, a typeface with a low contrast and strong serifs, led to TheAntiqua family. *"I started with TheSerif outlines, thinning thin parts, thickening thick parts, thereby enlarging the contrast."* (named revision A) That was not enough, more rigorous changes had to be made. This is Revision B in an ongoing design process. *"Surely this typeface family is not finished yet, I need another five years or so."* Licensing info: www.TheTypes.com

THEANTIQUAB-REGULAR 8 PT AT THIS SIZE some hint problems start to show. Those HP guys build nice printers, but should study type 1 hints a bit more. It looks like misinterpretation of ghost hints. Als ich wieder erwachte, spielten schon die ersten Morgenstrahlen an den grünen Vorhängen über mir. Ich könnte mich gar

THEANTIQUAB-REGULARCAPS IN TIME CONSUMING PROCESS OF BEING DESIGNED BY LUC(AS) DE GROOT, A DUTCH CHEESEHEAD. <HTTP://WWW.FONTFABRIK.COM> TOEN IK EINDELIJK WAKKER WERD VERDWEEN DE SLAPPE MIDDAGZON AL WEER BIJNA ACHTER

THEANTIQUAB-SEMIBOLD 6 PT HOW CAN ONE SET A LONGER TEXT in a slab serif font! Misuse of FFTheSerif, a typeface with a low contrast and strong serifs, led to TheAntiqua family. "I started with TheSerif outlines, thinning thin parts and thickening thick parts, thereby enlarging the contrast (revision A). That was not enough, more rigorous changes had to be made. This is Revision B in an ongoing process. Of course

THEANTIQUAB-BOLD 11 PT HOW CAN ONE SET A LONGER TEXT IN A SLAB SERIF FONT! MISUSE OF FFTHESERIF, a typeface with a low contrast and strong serifs, led to TheAntiqua family. *"I started with TheSerif outlines, thinning thin parts and thickening thick parts, thereby enlarging the contrast."* That was not enough, more rigorous changes had to be made. This is Revision B in an ongoing process. *"Of course*

THEANTIQUAB-SEMILIGHT 7 PT ALS ICH WIEDER ERWACHTE, spielten schon die ersten Morgenstrahlen an den grünen Vorhängen über mir. Ich könnte mich gar nicht besinnen, wo ich eigentlich wäre. Es kam mir vor, als führe ich noch immerfort im Wagen, und es hätte mir von einem Schlosse im Mondschein geträumt und von einer alten Hexe und ihrem blassen Töchterlein. Ich sprang endlich rasch *aus dem Bette, kleidete mich an, und sah mich dabei nach allen Seiten in dem Zimmer um. Da bemerkte ich*

THEANTIQUAB-REGULAR 5 PT ALS ICH WIEDER erwachte, spielten schon die ersten Morgenstrahlen an den grünen Vorhängen über mir. Ich könnte mich gar nicht besinnen, wo ich eigentlich wäre. Es kam mir vor, als führe ich noch immerfort im Wagen, und es hätte mir von einem Schlosse im Mondschein geträumt und von einer alten Hexe und ihrem blassen Töchterlein. Ich sprang endlich rasch aus dem Bette, kleidete mich an, und sah mich dabei nach allen Seiten in dem Zimmer um. Da bemerkte ich eine kleine Tapetentür, die ich gestern gar nicht gesehen

THEANTIQUAB-REGULAR 13 PT DE EXPORT BLIJFT QUA OMVANG typisch zwak. Ex-premier Jan de Quay was bovenal zelf geschokt. Felixje, Querido's uitgaven zijn wel prachtboeken. In Zweden vocht groepje quakers bij sexfilm. Ik gaf z'n quasi sexy vrouw acht bedlampjes. Jim zag de helft van de New York-Quebecexpres. Lex bederft uw quiz met typisch

Agrofont*

16 pt De meeste van onze Nederlandse huisvrouwen zijn er zo lang

14 pt zamerhand wel van doordrongen dat de groenten waar ons **vaderland** zo rijkelijk

12 pt mee bedeeld is, een schat van vitaminen en *fijne mineralen* bevatten. Vroeger werden groenten door velen als een

10 pt luxe, of als een min of meer noodzakelijk kwaad beschouwd. Maar nu denkt men daar heel anders over. *Minstens eenmaal per dag* verschijnt dit vitaminerijke
Release date: January 1st 2000
Info: <www.TheTypes.com>

Agrofont Mager
AaBbCcDdEeFfGg123
Mager cursief
AaBbCcDdEeFfGg456

Agrofont Normaal
HhIiJjKkLlMmNn789
Normaal cursief
HhIiJjKkLlMmNn012

Agrofont Vet
OoPpQqRrSs$£¢€ƒ
Vet cursief
OoPpQqRrSsß(§)?!&

***to be released as* AgroSans**

9 pt produkt op onze tafels. **Algemene bereidingswijze voor bladgroenten** Zorg er voor dat de groente zo vers mogelijk is. Groenten uit eigen tuin plukt men daarom zo kort mogelijk voor de bereiding, bij voorkeur wanneer ze niet in de zon staan. Een paar topjes voor grijze massa erbij.

8 pt Laat de groente na het kopen of plukken niet te lang en vooral niet op een warme plaats liggen. Verwijder alleen de delen, die verdord of aangestoken zijn. Was de groente zo vlug mogelijk in ruim water. Snij ze daarna pas fijn. Behandel vooral tere

6 pt Commisioned by the Dutch design bureau Studio Dumbar, Luc(as) developed a new sans serif typeface family for the Dutch *ministerie van landbouw, natuurbeheer en visserij.* Manually hinted True Type fonts are implemented throughout the ministery's many offices. *A expanded version of the family AgroSans will be made available for licensing at the start of the next century.*

5 pt Voeg alleen in gevallen van uiterste noodzaak wat zout aan het waswater toe en laat haar zo kort mogelijk hierin staan. De meeste van onze Nederlandse huisvrouwen zijn er zo langzamerhand wel van doordrongen, dat de groenten, waar ons vaderland zo rijkelijk mee bedeeld is, een schat van vitaminen en mineralen bevatten. Vroeger werden de groenten door velen als een luxe, of als een min of meer noodzakelijk kwaad beschouwd, maar nu denkt men daar heel anders.. A thoroughly hinted TrueType package will be available as well. Good heavens, that took so long to make! Design of the fonts: Luc(as) de Groot, <luc@fontfabrik.com>

18/22 De meeste van onze Nederlandse huisvrouwen ZWIJGEND BIKT MAX ELF HALVE CROQUETJES OP de groenten, waar ons **vaderland** zo rijkelijk mee bedeeld is, een schat van vitaminen & mineralen bevatten. 1998 *"De export blijft qua omvang typisch zwak."* **Felixje, Querido's uitgaven zijn wel prachtboeken!**

TYPEFACE

· · · · · · · · · · · · ·

Typeface Designer
Luc(as) de Groot
Berlin, Germany

· · · · · · · · · · · · ·

Foundry
TheTypes.com

· · · · · · · · · · · · ·

Client
Studio Dumbar

· · · · · · · · · · · · ·

Typeface Name
Agrofont

· · · · · · · · · · · · ·

Members of Typeface Family/System
Agrofont Light, Agrofont Light Italic, Agrofont Regular, Agrofont Regular Italic, Agrofont Bold, and Agrofont Bold Italic

Typeface Name
TheSansT

Members of Typeface Family/System
TheSansT Extra Light, TheSansT Light, TheSansT Semi Light, TheSansT Plain, TheSansT Semi Bold, TheSansT Bold, TheSansT Extra Bold, TheSansT Black, and eight italics

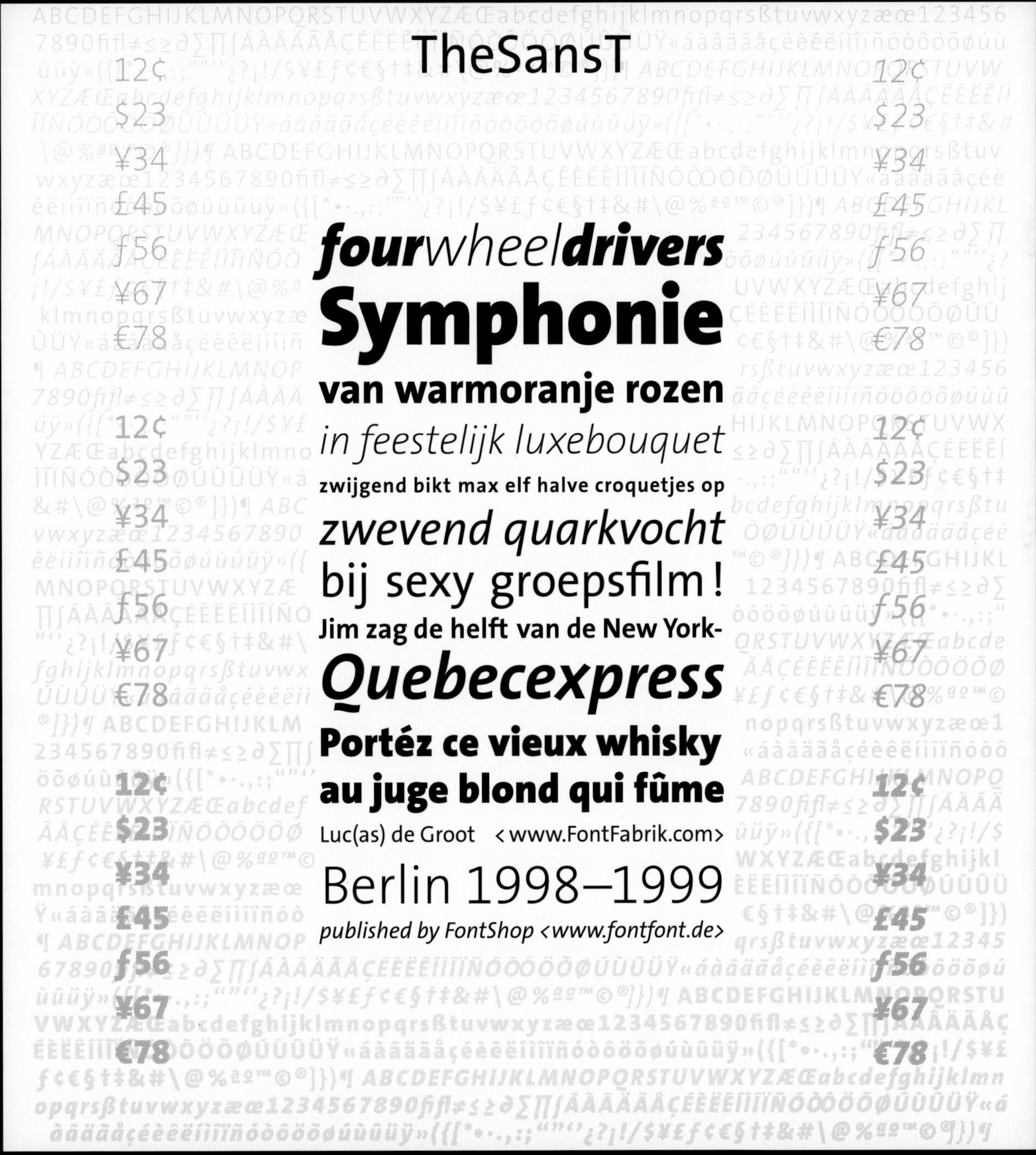

TheSansT

*four*wheel***drivers***

Symphonie

van warmoranje rozen

in feestelijk luxebouquet

zwijgend bikt max elf halve croquetjes op

zwevend quarkvocht

bij sexy groepsfilm!

Jim zag de helft van de New York-

Quebecexpress

Portéz ce vieux whisky au juge blond qui fûme

Luc(as) de Groot ‹ www.FontFabrik.com ›

Berlin 1998–1999

published by FontShop ‹www.fontfont.de›

TYPEFACE

Typeface Designer
Lee Schulz
Boston, Massachusetts

Typeface Name
Salomé

АБВГДЕЖЗИЙ
КЛМНОПРСТУФХЦ
ЧШЩЪЫЬЭЮЯ
абвгдежзийкл
мнопрстуфхцчш
щъыьэюя
1234567890

TYPEFACE

Typeface Designer
Yuri Gordon
Moscow, Russia

Foundry/Manufacturer
ParaType Ltd.

Typeface Name
FaRer Cyrillic

Language
Cyrillic

Year of Design or Release
1997

АБВГДЕЖЗИЙ

КЛМНОПРСТУФХЦ

ЧШЩЪЫЬЭЮЯ

абвгдежзийкл

мнопрстуфхцчш

щъыьэюя

1234567890

TYPEFACE
. . . .
Typeface Designer
Yuri Gordon
Moscow, Russia
. . . .
Foundry/Manufacturer
ParaType Ltd.
. . . .
Typeface Name
Dve Kruglyh Cyrillic
. . . .
Language
Cyrillic
. . . .
Year of Design or Release
1997

الله

للللٱٱٱٱٱٱٱٱٱللل إإٕإ اا ببب ب ت تتت
ثثث ج ججج ج ججهج ج خ خخخ
دد خذ خذ رررز رز رز سس سسسس
شش شش شش ش صص صط ططط
صض ضضض طط طط ظظظ ظظظ
عععع ع غغغغ ف ففف
ق ققق كءكءك كءك ل لللك مممم
ننن ن ةة ه هه ها ة ن و قـقـ يـيـيـي
كـئـئـئـ مـحـ
لإلإلإلأ لآلآلآلآ لالالا
لإلإلإ لإلإلإ

٠١٢٣٤٥٦٧٨٩

حرف ف بارتايب كوفي

TYPEFACE
· · · · · · · · · · ·
Typeface Designer
Lyubov Kuznetsova
Moscow, Russia
· · · · · · · · · · ·
Foundry/Manufacturer
ParaType Ltd.
· · · · · · · · · · ·
Typeface Name
PT Kufi Arabic
· · · · · · · · · · ·
Language
Arabic
· · · · · · · · · · ·
**Members of Typeface
Family/System**
PT Kufi Arabic Light,
PT Kufi Arabic Light
Oblique, PT Kufi Arabic
Regular, PT Kufi Arabic
Regular Oblique,
PT Kufi Arabic Bold,
and PT Kufi Arabic
Bold Oblique
· · · · · · · · · · ·
Year of Design or Release
1997

ԱԲԳԴԵՁԷԸ ԹԺԻԼԽԾԿՀՁՂՃՄ ՅՆՇՈՉՊՋՌՍՎ ՏՐՑԻՓՔՕՖ աբգդեզէըթժիլիծ կհծղճմյնշոչ պջռսվտրցւփքևօֆ 1234567890

TYPEFACE
. . . .

Typeface Designer
Manvel Shmavonyan
Moscow, Russia
. . . .

Foundry/Manufacturer
ParaType Ltd.
. . . .

Typeface Name
PT Margarit Armenian
. . . .

**Members of Typeface
Family/System**
PT Margarit Armenian Book,
PT Margarit Armenian Italic,
PT Margarit Armenian Bold,
and PT Margarit Armenian
Bold Italic
. . . .

Year of Design or Release
1997

▶

TYPEFACE
. . . .

Typeface Designer
Scott-Martin Kosofsky
(after Richard Austin,
London, 1788)
Boston, Massachusetts
. . . .

Typeface Name
Philidor Bell-Text
. . . .

**Members of Typeface
Family/System**
Philidor Bell-Text Roman,
Philidor Bell-Text Italic, and
Philidor Bell-Text Small
Caps
. . . .

**Year of Design or
Release**
1995

Size matters. Philidor Bell is a family designed for setting 11—12 point *text* with an alternate version made for setting 9–9½ point footnotes. No more, no less. Seeing it in *Typography 19* was something of a shock. The book's designer elected to show the types (the basic roman alphabet only) in a display setting, at around 48 pt. Its appearance was, in a word, hideous. Imagine a Levittown house enlarged to the size of the Taj Mahal or the Sistine Chapel reduced to the size of a New England saltbox. I find these frightening propositions, though some apparently disagree.

Why bother making distinctions? One reason is that reading is important and any text worth the effort should be presented without impediments. Bad proportions are surely a major problem, though it should be said that our reading habits are highly acculturated and the types that were considered easily readable in one era might seem uncomfortable in another. For example, I find Scotch and related moderns that were prevalent through most of the 19th century to be rather uncomfortable for reading over a long haul. I don't believe that they appeared so then. Be that as it may, each size was cut separately and good proportions and spacing were preserved throughout the range.

In our era, when an increasing amount of text is read on a video screen, the paradigms of readability are changing again and I believe they will continue to change until we've come full circle to the point at which video displays have the same visual texture as paper.

ABOUT PHILIDOR BELL: The family comprises a roman, an italic, and small caps. There is no bold (whose use I try assiduously to avoid). Like all my typeface designs, it was made for my own exclusive use, with its own hyphenation and justification algorithms. Bell originated with a specific book design project, in this case *Writing History: 150 Years of the A. T. Cross Company,* an in-depth history of the world's oldest writing instrument manufacturing company. The book was winner of the American Institute of Graphic Arts' Fifty Books / Fifty Covers of the Year of 1996.

It is by no means an "original" design. It was based on the 1788 Richard Austin types made for the publisher John Bell. Its most recent metal incarnation, made by the Monotype Corporation in the 1930s, was a beautiful rendering, though not satisfactory in all sizes. Much of my version is based on it, though I've also incorporated characters from the earlier, pre-machine set version called Brimmer by Bruce Rogers and Mountjoye by D. B. Updike. (It was identified as the Austin/Bell type by Stanley Morison.) The weight of Philidor Bell is based on the appearance of the Brimmer/Mountjoye type, adjusted for offset printing.

By the way, the larger type used here is Philidor Bell, with proportions adjusted in Illustrator.

—*Scott-Martin Kosofsky*

A

ABCDEFGH
IJKLMNOPQRSTUV
WXYZÆŒabcdefghijklm
nopqrstuvwxyz áèîöçñåÿfiflffi
fflffæœctst1234567890({[«·.,:;""'
?!$£¢¶§†‡&#\@%™©®»]})

PHILIDOR BELL
designed especially for text typesetting

by SCOTT-MARTIN KOSOFSKY *at*
The Philidor Company, Boston

ABCDEFGHIJKLMNOPQRSTU
VWXYZÆŒ abcdefghijklmnop
pqrstuvwxyz áèîöçñåÿ fiflffiffl
ffæœctst&1234567890 ABC
DEFGHIJKLMNOPQRS
TUVWXYZÆŒ

Z

Philidor Hillel ׃הלל פילידור

A HEBREW DISPLAY TYPE
DESIGNED IN 1991 BY SCOTT-MARTIN KOSOFSKY

בראשית

בָּרָא אלהים את השמים ואת הארץ׃

משנה תורה

חלק שני חיבר הנשר הגדול רבינו משה בן חדיין
רבי מיימון הספרדי זצ"ל.

ברכותת תלמוד בבלי

276 T D C 20

THE CHARACTER SET:

אבגדהוזחטיכךלמסנן סעפף צץקרשת
כבת ־ ־ ii . , ; ׃ 1234567890

TYPEFACE
· · · · · · · · · · · · ·
Typeface Designer
Scott-Martin Kosofsky
Boston, Massachusetts
· · · · · · · · · · · · ·
Typeface Name
Philidor Hillel
· · · · · · · · · · · · ·
Language
Hebrew
· · · · · · · · · · · · ·
**Year of Design or
Release**
1991

Officers and Members

Kristin Cleveland '98
Travis Cliett '53
Graham Clifford '98
Mahlon A. Cline* '48
Tom Cocozza '76
Lisa Cohen '93
Stuart Cohen '96
Angelo Colella '90
Ed Colker '83
Marshall L.
Collins III '96
Maren Connary '98s
Kyle Cooper '97
Heather Corcoran '98s
Rodrigo Corral '98
Madeleine Corson '96
Lynette Cortez '99
Cara Costa '97s
Tony Costellano '97
Susan Cotler-Block '89
Bradley Wilde
Cranshaw II '96
Freeman Craw* '47
Bart Crosby '95
Jeff Culver '97s
Glen Cummings '98s
David Cundy '85
Brian Cunningham '96
Jennifer Curtiss '98s
Rick Cusick '89
Michael Damare '98
Brian Daniels '98s
Robert de Vicq de
Cumptich '97
Susan Darbyshire '87
Jim Darilek '98
Don Davidson '93
Richard Dawson '93
Einat Lisa Day '97s
Rena DeBortolo '97
Matej Decko '93
Paige De Leo '98
Josanne De Natale '86
Phil Delbourgo '98
Ernst Dernehl '87
Jeannie Detter '96
Ray Diaz '97s
Ray Diaz '98
W. Brian Diecks '98
Claude A. Dieterich '84
Joseph DiGioia '96
Jeanette Wilkinson
Dill '99
Cohava Dodo '97s
Tom Dolle '95
Seth Dominck '97s
Jonathan Doney '96
Lou Dorfsman '54
Cheri Dorr '97
Pascale Dovic '97
Stephen Doyle '98
John Dreyfus** '68
Christopher
Dubber '85
Kay Duncan '97s
Jeffrey Dunn '98
Rod Durso '98
Simon Dwelly '98
Lutz Dziarnowski '92
Anna Egger-
Schlesinger '98

Rick Eiber '85
Friedrich
Eisenmenger '93
Jeani Eismont '96
Lise Ellingson '98s
Dr. Elsi Vassdal Ellis '93
Garry Emery '93
Bob English '97
Elke Erschfeld '99
Joseph Michael
Essex '78
Greg Evans '98
Leslie Evans '92
Florence Everett '89
John Fahey '98s
Peter Fahrni '93
Jan Fairbairn '97
Simon Fairweather '96
Dug Falby '99
Chen Fang '95
David Farey '93
Michael Farmer '94
Erik Faulhaber '97s
Gene Federico** '91
Antero Ferreira '97
Simon Fitton '94
Kristine Fitzgerald '90
Roberta Fitzgerald '97
Janet Flessland '98
Norbert Florendo '97
Gonçalo Fonseca '93
Wayne Ford '96
Thomas Fowler '93
Alessandro
Franchini '96
Carol Freed '87
Kaye Frost-Hunt '97
Adrian Frutiger** '67
Mario Fuhr '97
Angela Fung '98
Yoko Furuichi '97s
Gene Gable '95
Christopher
Galvin '99s
Luciana J. Garcia '98s
Meredith Garniss '98
Christof Gassner '90
Martina Gates '96s
David Gatti '81
Jeremy Gee '92
Kai Gehrmann '96s
Leah Gernert '97
Robyn Gill-Attaway '93
Robert Givens '96
Lou Glassheim* '47
Howard Glener '77
Rüdiger Goetz '95
Carin Goldberg '97
Lorenz Goldnagl '99s
Ronnen Goren '97
Holly Goscinsky '98s
Edward Gottschall '52
Norman Graber '69
Diana Graham '85
Austin Grandjean '59
Stephen Green '97
Karen Greenberg '95
Roger Greiner '96
Adam Greiss '89
Risa Greiss '94
James Grieshaber '96

Jeff Griffith '91
Phill Grimshaw '96
Ciaran Groarke '97s
Frank E. E. Grubich '96
Rosanne Guararra '92
Christiane Gude '97
Stephan
Guggenbichler '97
Edith Gutierrez '97s
Olga Gutierrez
de la Roza '95s
Einar Gylfason '95
Peter Gyllan '97
Doug Haden '97
William Hafeman '96
Allan Haley '78
Crystal Hall '97
Debra Hall '96
Doug Hall '99s
Everett Halvorsen '98
Keith Harris '98
Theodore Harrison '96
Knut Hartmann '85
Helen Hayes '98
Bonnie Hazelton '75
Jeri Heiden '94
Frank Heine '96
Wild Heinz '96
Robyn Hepker '97
Earl M. Herrick '96
Klaus Hesse '95
Fons M. Hickmann '96
Sally Hiesiger '98
Jay Higgins '88
Pamela Hill '96
Helmut Himmler '96
Norihiko Hirata '96
Michelle Hoagland '98
Brian Hodge '98
J. Drew Hodges '95
Michael Hodgson '89
Cynthia Hoffman '96
Catherine
Hollenbeck '93
Maria
Honigmann '97s
Kevin Horvath '87
Lauren House '97
Tonya Hudson '99
Gerard Huerta '85
David Hukari '95
Harvey Hunt '92
Theresa
Hutchison '98s
M. Iqbal '99
Terry Irwin '96
Donald Jackson** '78
Jim Jackson '98
Michael Jager '94
John Jamilkowski '97
Iskra Johnson '94
Andy Johnson '99
E. R. Johnson '98s
Margo Johnson '99
Vasken Kalayjian '96
Jeff Kalin '96
John Kallio '96
Rosanne Kang '98
Kelly Kao '98
Maryann Karr
Saggese '96

Moshe Kasman '97s
Shigeo Katsuoka '97
Koji Katsuta '97s
Carolyn Kaufman '99
Ronan Keane '99
Nan Keeton '97
Stacey Kelley '97
Bostijan Botas
Kenda '98
Russell Kerr '98s
Richard Keyler '96
Kay Khoo '99
Jang Hoon Kim '97s
Linda Kim '98
Rick King '93
Brandie Kirkman '98s
Robert C. Knecht '69
Kayleen Knipper '96
Alexander Knowlton '96
Cynthia Knox '95
Nana Kobayashi '94
Claus Koch '96
Jesse Taylor
Koechling '98s
Patricia Koh '97s
Kwan Shunn Kong '98
Steve Kopec '74
Matthias Kott '96s
Katharina Kramer '99s
Andrej Krátky '93
Marcus Kraus '97
Philip Krayna '97
Bernhard J. Kress '63
Christian Kunnert '97
Ralf Kunz '93
Kuang Chun Kuo '97s
Yoshiko Kusaka '97s
Jin Hee Kwon '98s
Gerry L'Orange '91
Raymond F. Laccetti '87
Angela Lai '99
John Langdon '93
Guenter Gerhard
Lange '83
Yerje Laneggen '98
Amanda Lawrence '99
Lana Le '98
Katherine Lee '96
Susan Lee '97s
Judith Kazdym Leeds '83
David Lemon '95
Maru Leon '96
Olaf Leu '65
James Wai Mo Leung '97
Debby W. Levin '96
Janet Levinson '96
Adam Levite '97
Renee Levitt '98s
Nir Levy '98s
Robyn Lewis '97
Martin Liao '97s
Chun-Chien Lien '97
Miles Linklater '98
Lawrence Lipkin '97s
David Lippman '96s
Monica Little '98
Wally Littman '60
Esther Liu '98
Boris Ljubicic '97
Lorena Llaneza '98s
Uwe Loesch '96

Beverly Logan '97s
Catriona
Lohan-Conway '97
John Howland
Lord** '47
Melinda S. Love '96
Pei-Yu Lu '97s
Alexander Luckow '94
Kristine Luhrssen '98
Gregg Lukasiewicz '90
Katherine Lynch '98
Monib Mahdavi '96s
Sol Malkoff '63
Marilyn Marcus '79
Ari Mardewi '97s
Marie Mariucci '98
Rosemary
Markowsky '98s
David Marshall '98
Linda Martin '96s
Adolfo Martinez '86
Frank Martinez '99
Rogério Martins '91
Igor Masnjak '98
Les Mason '85
Michelle Mason '97
Willie Mathis '96s
Andreas Maxbauer '95
Douglas May '92
Caroline McAlpine '99
Sherwood McBloom '96
Barbara McCullough '97
Rod McDonald '95
Tony M. McEachern '99
Malcolm McGaughy '96
Marc A. Meadows '96
Roland Mehler '92
Frédéric Metz '85
David Michaelides '97
Tony Mikolajczyk '97
Reggie Milbern '97
Andrew Miller '96
Jennifer Miller '98
Michael Milley '95
John Milligan '78
Elena Miranda '97s
Michael Miranda '84
Oswaldo Miranda
(Miran) '78
Ralf Mischnick '98s
Susan L. Mitchell '96
Carrie Monaco '97s
Robin Locke Monda '96
Sakol
Mongkolkasetarin '95
Steve Monsosson '96
James Montalbano '93
Joseph Montebello '96
Jennifer Moore '98s
Richard Moore '82
Alexa Morgenstern '98s
Minoru Morita '75
John Morris '98
Tobias Moss* '47
Pete Muhlenberg '98
Richard Mullen '82
Joachim Müller-
Lancé '95
Lars Müller '97
Gary Munch '97
Antonio Muñoz '90

Darrell Munro '97
Jerry King Musser '88
Alexander Musson '93
Louis A. Musto '65
Norikazu Nakamura '99s
Nathan Nedorostek '98s
Cristiana
    Neri-Downey '97
Robert Newman '96
Thu Nguyen '98s
Maria Nicholas '96s
Katherine Nichols '96
Shuichi Nogami '97
Gillian R. Norrie '97
Christopher Norris '98
Robert Norton '92
Alexa Nosal '87
Michelle Novak '97
Robert Nuell '97s
Richard O'Connell '99
Oisin O'Malley '98s
Kevin O'Sullivan '97
Mary Alice O'Toole '96
Mariele
    Obersteiner '97s
Jack Odette '77
Nina V. Oertzen '99
Judith Ohayon '96
Akio Okumara '96
Mark Oldach '96
Michel Olivier '94
Nancy Ovedovitz '96
Robert Overholtzer '94
Rebecca Ozaki '96
Toshi Ozone '95s
Frank Paganucci '85
Robert Palmer '96
Deborah Pang '99
A. Samantha
    Panzier '97s
Aubree Pappas '98s
Enrique Pardo '99
Jean Park '99s
Steven Seung
    Ik Park '97s
Sam Park '98s
Jim Parkinson '94
Guy Pask '97
Babita Patel '99s
Jayesh Patel '97
Jane Patterson '98
Cherly Paulin '96
Gudrun Pawelke '96
Melanie Paykos '96
Christi Payne '96
B. Martin Pedersen '85
Daniel Pelavin '92
Tamaye Perry '98
Mikko Petäjä '96
Robert Peters '86
Ronnie Peters '97
Oanh Pham-Phu '96
Clive Piercy '96
Renee Platt '91
William Porch '94
Richard Poulin '97
Lisa Powers '96s
Will Powers '89
Vaneerat
    Pramongkit '99s
Vittorio Prina '88

James Propp '97
Anita Pucinischi '98s
Richard Puder '85
Burt Purmell '98
David Quay '80
Christine Rae '96
Erwin Raith '67
Zeljko Rajacic '99
Bob Rauchman '97
Marco Ravanetti '99
Nema Ray '97s
Jo Anne Redwood '88
Hans Dieter Reichert '92
Liz Reitman '97
James T. Rhoades '99
Ian Richer '98s
Robert Rindler '95
Phillip Ritzenberg '97
Nadine Robbins '95
Eva Roberts '96
Helen Roberts '98s
William W. Robinson '96
Frank Rochell '99
Elizabeth Rodriguez '97
Tim Rolands '96
Salvadore Romero '94
Hoet Ronane '99
Edward Rondthaler* '47
Wendy Ronga '96
Kurt Roscoe '93
Elizabeth Rovnick '96
Erkki Ruuhinen '86
Timothy J. Ryan '96
Michael Rylander '93
Eric Saari '99s
Gus Saelens '50
Stephanie Sakai '97s
David Saltman '66
Ina Saltz '96
Anthony Salvo '96
Diana Salzburg '98
Aleya Anil Samji '98s
Rodrigo Sanchez '96
Susan Sanderson '96
Stephanie Sassola-
    Struse '97
Kaoru Sawada '97s
Frank Sax '94
John Sayles '95
David Saylor '96
Matthias Schäfer '97s
Hermann J. Schlieper '87
Hermann Schmidt '83
Klaus Schmidt '59
Markus Schmidt '93
Bertram Schmidt-
    Friderichs '89
Helmut Schmitt-
    Siegel '97
Werner Schneider '87
Geraldine Schoeller '96
Curtis Schreiber '97
Eileen Hedy Schultz '85
Lauren Schultz '98s
Eckehart Schumacher-
    Gebler '85
Christian Schwartz '95s
Jo Scraba '97s
James Sebastian '95
Heather Seeley '97
Anri Seki '97s

Enrico Sempi '97
Kathryn Shagas '97
Jessica Shatan '95
Paul Shaw '87
Lisa Sheirer '96
Leslie Sherr '96a
Kim Shkapich '97
Philip Shore, Jr. '92
Bergdis
    Sigurdardottio '98
Susan Silton '96
Mark Simkins '92
Scott Simmons '94
Todd Simmons '97
Arlyn Simon '95
Mondrey Sin '95
Edward Sinn '97
Mae Skkidmore '98
Pat Sloan '97
Jamie Slomski '98
Cara Snell '97s
Felix Sockwell '95
Silvestre
    Segarra Soler '95
Martin Solomon '55
Jan Solpera '85
Mark Solsburg '89
Ronnie Tan
    Soo Chye '88
Brian Sooy '98
Erik Spiekermann '88
Vic Spindler '73
Julie Spivey '98s
Randy Squeo '98s
Randy Stano '96
Rolf Staudt '84
Thomas Stecko '94
Olaf Stein '96
Jennifer Sterling '96
Charles Stewart '92
Sumner Stone '88
William Streever '50
Ilene Strizver '88
Matthew J. Strong '98s
Vance Studley '95
Katja Stuke '97
Hansjorg Stulle '87
Alissa Sturm '97s
Gregor Stute '98s
Meena Sukhyanga '98s
Zempaku Suzuki '92
Paul Sych '93
Laurie Szujewska '95
Kan Tai-Keung '97
Douglas Tait '98
Yukichi Takada '95
Hirohiko Takahashi '98
Yoshimaru Takahashi '96
Akiko Takai '97s
Jef Tan '96
Lilian Tang '97
William Taubin '56
Jack Tauss '75
Lisa Marie Taylor '97
Michael Taylor '96
Pat Taylor '85
Anthony J. Teano '62
Ana Teixeira '98s
Mark Tenga '93
Danielle Termini '98s
Regine Thienhaus '96

George H. Thomas '98
Dana Thompson '98
Trevor Thompson '97s
Wayne Tidswell '96
Fred Tieken '95
Eric Tilley '95
Colin Tillyer '97
Anton Tilo '98
Laura Tolkow '96
Joseph Treacy '94
Lynn-Ann Truchon '98s
Doros Tsolakis '97
Akihiko Tsukamoto '97
James Tung '97s
François Turcotte '99
Michael Tutino '96
Kate Ulanov '95
Camille Utterback '97s
Edward Vadala '72
Diego Vainesman '91
Sandra Horvat
    Vallely '97
Christine Van Bree '98
Mark van Bronkhorst '93
Kevin van der Leek '97
Jan Van Der Ploeg '52
Elexis Van Reen '97
Trisha Mitchell
    Vargas '97s
Yuri Vargas '99
Ané Vecchione '97s
Anna Villano '99s
Annette von Brandis '96
Thilo von Debschitz '95
Alex Voss '98
Scott Wadler '95
Bob Wages '96
Frank Wagner '94
Allan R. Wahler '98
Chee Wai '97s
Jurek Wajdowicz '80
Sergio Waksman '96
Susan Waksmonski '96
Garth Walker '92
Donna M.
    Walker '97s
Xu Wang '93
Jane Ward '98s
Kurt Watson '99
Jessica Watts '99
Janet Webb '91
Matt Weber '98s
Edmund Wee '97
Joy Weeeng '93s
Kurt Weidemann '66
Claus F.
    Weidmueller '97
Yukiko Weissenfluh '99s
Judy Wert '96a
John D. Westgate '96
Paul Wharton '96
Alex White '93
Scott White '99
Albert L. Whitley, Jr. '98s
Bambang Widodo '98
Richard Wilde '93
James Williams '88
Joseph R. Williams '98s
Carol Winer '94
Conny J.Winter '85
Penina Wissner '96

Delve Withrington '97
Peter C. Wong '96
Anuthin
    Wongsunkakon '98s
Andrew Wood '98
Peter Wood '97
Fred Woodward '95
Laura Coe Wright '99
Chien Hui Yang '98s
Lynn Yeo '98s
Doyald Young '96
Adrienne Youngstein '97
Alicia Zanzinger '96
Hermann Zapf** '52
Maxim Zhukov '96
Piotr Zmuda '98s
Roy Zucca '69
Jeff Zwerner '97

SUSTAINING MEMBERS

Adobe Systems,
Inc. '90

Agfa, Division Bayer
Corporation '96

Galapagos Design
Group, Inc. '96

International Typeface
Corporation '80

Letraset '91

Monotype
Typography, Inc. '91

*..........Charter member
**.....Honorary member
s..........Student member
a.......Associate member

Membership as
of May 31, 1999

For membership
information please
contact the
Type Directors Club.

Type Directors Club
60 East 42nd Street
Suite 721
New York, New York
10165
Tel: 212-983-6042
Fax: 212-983-6043
E-mail: director@tdc.org
Web site: www.tdc.org

Carol Wahler
Executive Director

General Index

ăn'nū̇al *a.* & *n.* **1.** *a.* reckoned by the year; recurring yearly (~ **ring,** ring in cross-section of tree, fish, etc., from one year's growth); lasting for one year; hence ~**LY²** *adv.*